Antidote For the Guilt of Sin

Justification By Faith Alone

Martin Murphy

Antidote For the Guilt of Sin

Published by: Theocentric Publishing
4827 County Road 6
Selma, Alabama   36701

http://www.theocentricpublishing.com

ISBN 9781733454070

This book is dedicated to the future pastors and teachers who will faithfully teach the doctrine of justification by faith alone.

Foreword

Just when I thought Martin Murphy could not outdo himself as an author, he has proven me wrong. This is the best book he has written, and is by far the most cogent and clear teaching of the doctrine of Justification by Faith Alone that I have read.

And what better way to present the truth of Justification by Faith Alone than by an exposition of the first five chapters of Romans. Murphy in this work dives into all the aspects of saving faith. There is a wealth of information here and many questions will be answered from these pages.

This doctrine, as perhaps the most oft-repeated and conspicuous statement of the Protestant Reformation, sorely needs expounding in our day. When spoken of, the term is typically a byword, which has no content for many. To those who believe it only means mental assent, or antinomian freedom, or "praying the sinners' prayer," they will be thoroughly debunked by Martin Murphy in these pages.

At the same time, in the last chapter of this book, he compares the difference between James and Paul's approach to faith vs. works and shows how they do not contradict but are entirely compatible, and emphasizes that faith always produces works.

Nor does he shy away from the subject of the wrath of God, a landscape where many fear to tread, which is antithetic to the feel-good, "seeker- friendly" church culture today. Yet this theme is crucial in Romans and without grasping that and the purpose of the Law, there is little hope in understanding why justification by faith alone is so important.

There is nothing obscure or vague here, and there is a minimum of theological technical terms that might require a dictionary for the lay reader. At the same time, it is not so simplified that it compromises or waters down the truth of God's word. Murphy combines a theologically deep and profound exposition of the subject, yet with language and logic that can be understood by most believers.

N. G. Rudulph, Jr.
Pastor

Table of Contents

Introduction

The dumbing down of the evangelical church took place over a long period of time. There is no quick fix to this sad commentary. Pastors and teachers tried to simplify Bible doctrine so that children could understand. The children became adults, but they never matured in sound biblical doctrine. They forgot to "Hold fast the pattern of sound words which you have heard from me (the Apostle Paul), in faith and love which are in Christ Jesus" (2 Timothy 1:13).

Serious Bible study is often despised in the contemporary church. Unfortunately, many Sunday School teachers and pastors teach heresy to a greater or lesser degree on a regular basis. They either do not understand correct biblical doctrine or they may be afraid to teach it. It is still the responsibility of the church to teach its members what to believe and how to live according to biblical standards. A flimsy, pietistic, cursory, understanding of the Word of God is a shame and disgrace for any professing Christian. Even those who do study the Bible often have no concern for consistency and coherency. Christians must carefully study the Word of God, so they will accurately understand the will of God.

Corruption, fraud, and deceit have and always will exist until the Lord returns for His church. Christians should disenfranchise themselves from the evils of this age and live carefully and accurately according to the Word of God. Paul commanded the Ephesian Church to "redeem the time." Make the most of the time God has given you. I hate it when people tell me the church cannot be reformed. That is contrary to the Word of God. The phrase in Ephesians chapter 5 verse 16 "redeeming the time" literally means "buy up the time." Redeeming the time has nothing to do with gaining time or losing time. You can't create one extra moment for your life and Satan cannot steal one moment from your life. God has ordained how many minutes we have to serve Him and nothing can change His ordination. Redeeming the time has to do with making the best use of every circumstance as God providentially brings it your way. Maximize your gifts! (*Exposition of Ephesians*, by Martin Murphy, pg. 110)

The Bible is a storehouse of knowledge, moral instruction and godly principles, none of which should be ignored. However, the center of attention is Jesus Christ. Although the Word of God reveals many "incomparable excellences" it reveals "the only way of man's salvation." The word "salvation" is appropriate to describe a holy God having a favorable relationship with sinful human beings. The church has failed to teach the unique doctrine that turns an unfavorable relationship into a favorable relationship. It is my purpose in this book to explain the doctrine of Scripture relative to "justification by faith alone." I will endeavor to accomplish this task with a careful study of the first 5 chapters of the book of Romans.

Although my work will be expressed as an exposition of Romans, the doctrine of justification by faith alone will shine like a bright star. Justification is an act of God so that God declares the believer righteous. God judges the believer to be innocent based on the imputed righteousness of Christ. Justification is found in the Old Testament (Genesis 15:6) and the New Testament (Romans 5:1).

This book is not an academic commentary of Romans. However, it is an exposition of the first 5 chapters of Romans with an eye on the doctrine of justification by faith alone. The central person in this exposition is Jesus Christ. The central doctrine is justification by faith alone.

1. Paul the Teacher of Justification by Faith

Romans 1:1-7

The city of Tarsus, located in a Roman province, was the birthplace of Paul. His Jewish family was of the tribe of Benjamin and he was a Roman citizen. Probably a contemporary of Jesus Christ, he called himself the son of a Pharisee. Tarsus, a prosperous city, was known for its emphasis on education, intellectual pursuits, and schools of rhetoric. Also, it was known as the center of Stoic philosophy. Stoicism is a system of philosophy that teaches self-salvation through knowledge. Some early Christian philosophers tried to integrate certain tenets of Stoicism into the Christian religion. In the words of the Roman historian and philosopher Strabo, "The people at Tarsus have devoted themselves so eagerly, not only to philosophy, but also to the whole round of education in general that they have surpassed even Athens or Alexandria." Since he spent his early years in Tarsus, Paul very likely understood the Roman culture, its religion, philosophy and apologetic.

Paul mentions his family only once in Romans 16:13: "Greet Rufus, a choice man in the Lord, his mother and mine (mother of Paul and of me)." Somewhere around the age of 14 Paul went to Jerusalem to study under the great Hebrew Rabbi Gamaliel, the grandson of Hillel. He was also educated by the philosophers at Tarsus since he makes mention of them in Acts 17:18 and Titus 1:12. Obviously he was trained in the school of rhetoric as evidenced by such New Testament writings as Acts 26:24-28. Then, he studied for 10 years after he was converted in preparation for the gospel ministry.

However, he spent most of his adult life earning a living making tents.

Paul's given Hebrew name was Saul, but he assumed the name Paul, a Gentile name, shortly after he began his mission to the Gentiles. Perhaps it denoted his desire to propagate the universal religion of Christianity, rather than the parochial religion of the Hebrews. The universal religion of Paul is one of the best proofs available for the Christian religion. Paul's epistles enabled the church to formulate a systematic theology.

Professing Christians may say, "I don't follow the teaching of any man." Poor souls don't even believe the Christian religion, because if Christians follow the teaching of Paul they are following the religion of a man named Paul who received his instruction from the divine man Jesus.

Christianity assumed its place around 33 A.D. as a small sect that came out of Judaism. By 65 A. D. Christianity was a world religion and in time would saturate the world. The historical growth of Christianity is to a great degree the result of the ministry of the man named Paul.

Christians have different gifts and abilities that should be nurtured, but they forget those are gifts and not self-achievements. Like the apostle Paul, Christians should desire to be called a slave of Jesus Christ.

The Psalmist said it well when he said:

> O Lord, truly I am Your servant; I am Your servant, the son of Your maidservant; You have loosed my bonds. I will offer to You the sacrifice of thanksgiving, And will call upon the name of the Lord. (Psalm 116:16ff)

Now put yourself in the place of these Roman Christians receiving this letter. Try to imagine that you lived in cosmopolitan Rome at the time Paul wrote this letter. It was about as wicked a place to live as any you could imagine today.

How would you feel at the reading of the first line of Paul's letter? "Paul a slave of Jesus Christ." Did they ask the question "Is Paul crazy?" What if one of those Christians was a slave? Free man or slave they were probably startled when Paul called himself a slave. Who wants to be a slave? No one unless the institution functions according to God's Law. However, under God's Law it is not a bad institution but, if perfected, it appears that Paul prefers biblical slavery over against secular freedom. Later in the letter to the Romans Paul will explain that Christians must be enslaved in order to be free.

Paul, the slave, was called to be an apostle. The noble call of an apostle never preceded the real effectual call of God to bring Paul into a state of salvation. Paul's effectual call to salvation and his call as an apostle are inseparable. The Bible confirms this doctrine:

> But when it pleased God who separated me from my mother's womb and called me through His grace to reveal His Son in me that I might preach Him among the Gentiles. (Galatians 1:15)

Paul was not ignorant of his unique call to the ministry: "For I consider that I am not at all inferior to the most eminent apostles" (2 Corinthians 11:5). Just think, the eminent apostle Paul was a slave. The slave was called to be an apostle.

Paul had a particular call to serve as an apostle. What does the word apostle mean? The word "apostle" comes from the Greek noun αποστολοσ (pronounced *apostolos*) which has its origin in the Greek verb αποστελλω (pronounced *apostello*), which is a compound verb. απο is the preposition that means "from" thus "send away." The main verb is στελλω (pronounced *stello)*, which means to arrange or to prepare.

These words were used as military metaphors meaning "line up." Literally the word apostle means "to send prepared." So the word apostle essentially means that someone has been prepared, qualified and has been given full power to act as the personal representative of the one sending him. The stress is on the one who does the sending, because the one sending has the authority to send. Obviously the sender would prepare the one who is sent.

The primary function of the apostle was not church politics, not church growth strategy, not living a happy healthy and prosperous life, but the primary function was to preach the gospel. He was called an apostle, but set apart for the gospel of God. Paul even asserts, under inspiration from God, "For Christ did not send me to baptize, but to preach the gospel. . ." (1 Corinthians 1:17).

The word "gospel" literally refers to a good announcement. The good announcement from God is good news. It is good news that since all people are sinners, God forgives sinners. Therefore, it is good news that sinners are saved by grace; justified by faith alone.

One of the best ways to make Christ the Lord in your life is for you to assume the posture of a slave, serving a perfect master. Christ summoned the church to enter into this great calling, submissively like a slave, but with the dignity of one sent forth by God as a royal ambassador.

2. Paul's Desire to Preach the Gospel

Romans 1:8-15

It is necessary to examine the historical context leading to the development of justification by faith alone. Paul understood his covenant relationship with God as it is clearly established in the Word of God. "I will establish My covenant between Me and you and your descendants after you in their generations, for an everlasting covenant" (Genesis 17:7). Paul further noted, "if you are Christ's, then you are Abraham's seed, and heirs according to the promise" (Galatians 3:29).

All religious worship and thanksgiving should be offered to God through Jesus Christ (1 Timothy 2:5). Paul says essentially the same thing in Ephesians 5:20. He gave thanks to God the Father in the name of our Lord Jesus Christ. Christians are specially bound to give thanks to God through Jesus Christ for those who have received the same grace. Paul's introductory remarks in his letter to the Roman church include a prayer of thanksgiving. Paul's reason for this prayer plants the seed for the remainder of this book. He prayed because of their faith. He did not pray that God would give them faith. He prayed with thanksgiving for their faith. Since faith is the gift of God, Christians, like the inspired apostle Paul must give thanks for God's gift. "For by grace you have been saved through faith, and that not of yourselves; it is the gift of God. . ." (Ephesians 2:8). However, good works are not merely desirable, they are necessary.

> A city that is set on a hill cannot be hidden. Nor do they light a lamp and put it under a basket, but on a lampstand, and it gives light to all who are in the house. Let your light so shine before men, that they

may see your good works and glorify your Father in heaven. (Matthew 5:14-16)

There is the danger of hypocrisy, if professing Christians pretend they have saving faith when they do not have saving faith. The sad truth is the church overflows with those who want others to think that they have a right standing with God, when they actually do not have that right standing. For that reason the church must teach the doctrine of justification by faith alone.

Paul was anxious to visit professing Christians at the various churches. "For I long to see you" (Romans 1:11). The verb is translated elsewhere "yearn for" (2 Corinthians 9:14). To the church at Philippi Paul wrote, "For God is my witness, how greatly I long for you all with the affection of Jesus Christ" (Philippians 1:8). A tender, but passionate expression from one who loved the people of God. He not only loved them, he wanted to minister to them. Again in Paul's letter to the Romans Paul wrote, "I planned to come to you, but was hindered" (Romans 1:13). This is the supreme example of a man who understands and finds comfort in the providence of God.

But there were intervening historical contingencies. Something happened that kept him from going to Rome. The providence of God is the factor to be reckoned when we think in terms of our plans and what we think is best.

Paul understood the biblical concept of providence. He knew that God's plans may not be the same as his plans. Paul knew that what God ordained, God sustains. Then God concurrently brings about His perfect will in a sinful world. Think about all the factors that God has to orchestrate to bring about the final result.

One event leads to another by a perfectly natural sequence in a sinful world. Satan's temptations and clever sophistries are merely character building events that help Christians understand God's plans.

When our plans are frustrated, we must do what we are able to do. It is always best to do the duty, which is nearest to your hand. God will cause "all things to work together for good to those who love God and are called according to His purpose" (Romans 8:28).

Paul had a social disposition that was part of his whole passion to go to Rome, but we know from the content and tone of his letter that he had a greater purpose for wanting to go to Rome. The apostle wanted to witness firsthand that which he had heard about the church at Rome.

There are three other reasons Paul desired to go to Rome.

1. Share a spiritual gift (Romans 1:11).
2. To see the church at Rome established (Romans 1:11).
3. To see the fruit of his ministry to the Romans (Romans 1:13).

John Wycliffe rendered the words "spiritual gift" as "spiritual grace" probably because the Greek word χαρισμα (pronounced *charisma*) is certainly associated with God's grace. Paul may have miraculous gifts in mind; however, the immediate context seems to militate against the necessity of performing miraculous gifts as a means for making disciples.

The question is: What gift did they need? What gift would strengthen their faith? What gift would be the most fruitful for the kingdom of God? These and many other questions would guide the apostle in his quest to encourage and strengthen the church at Rome. Paul did not devote his time and effort to plan frivolous events for the local church. Contemporary church revivals, conferences, and seminars abound and most of them are functionally useless relative to making disciples.

The context seems to militate against miraculous gifts as a means for making disciples. Paul expected Christians to use the gifts that are natural to the individual. To the church at Corinth Paul said, "Each one has his own gift from God, one in this manner and another in that" (1 Corinthians 7:7). Christians should encourage one another by the mutual faith they have, unless particular spiritual gifts are employed for that purpose.

Another reason for Paul's desire to go to Rome was to see the church established at Rome. The attention given to the Roman Christians was that they may be established or confirmed as disciples of Christ. The aorist passive infinitive indicates that the Romans are the recipients of the action. The emphasis was on the sovereign work of God establishing a person in the faith by the act of regeneration, which is followed by the work that God does in them.

Even so, God uses instruments to accomplish His purposes. Obviously Paul wanted to be an instrument in confirming the faith of the Roman Christians. Paul wanted God to work through him for the benefit of the church, which was a noble goal.

Paul the preacher/teacher would use the Word of God to strengthen the Roman Christians just like pastors use the Word of God to strengthen Christians under their care. The Southern Presbyterian theologian William Plumer made an astute observation based on this text.

> The strongest follower of Christ is as weak as water, except as his ways and principles are confirmed and strengthened by divine truth and all-sufficient grace constantly ministered to him.

The only way Christians find strength in this life is by understanding the nature and character of God in relation to the sinfulness of man. Therefore, a Mediator is necessary to reconcile sinful man and the holy God of heaven and earth. "For there is one God and one Mediator between God and men, the Man Christ Jesus (1 Timothy 2:5).

Ancillary to the other reasons for Paul wanting to go to Rome, there is one other found in Romans 1:13: "that I might have some fruit among you also." What does Paul mean by fruit? From his words at the end of verse 13 he expects the same thing from the Roman Christians that he had seen in the other predominately Gentile churches. "But the fruit of the Spirit is love, joy, peace, longsuffering, kindness, goodness, faithfulness, gentleness, self-control" (Galatians 5:22). Paul prayed for the Colossian Christians that "they might bear fruit in every good work."

If Christians expect to bear fruit for the kingdom of God, they have to be filled with the Spirit of God. They have to be strengthened by God's Spirit and they must have knowledge of God's will. The Scripture has set forth responsibilities to share spiritual gifts so the church may be strengthened in the faith. In the providence of God Christians may not get what they think they want, but their desire should be to see fruit in their labors.

Paul's passion to go to Rome is obviously a passion in his soul.

> I am a debtor both to Greeks and to barbarians, both to wise and the unwise. So, as much as is in me, I am ready to preach the gospel to you who are in Rome also. (Romans 1:14-15)

When you read, do you try to visualize the expressions of the writer? You should. Facial expression, body movement, the tone of the voice and other gestures or techniques is extremely important. They all help the hearer interpret the speaker. The writer will very likely use certain grammatical devices intended to guide the reader in the interpretation of the text.

Such is the case in Romans 1:14. The subject and verb "I am" are last in the word order of the sentence in the Greek text. It is placed last in the sentence to place emphasis on the subject and verb. Paul wanted to emphasize his state of being. He explains that he is under obligation. The Greek word οφειλετης (pronounced *opheiletes*) is translated "debtor" in the *New King James Version* and under obligation in the *New American Standard Version*. Paul emphasizes the fact that he was a debtor, since he referred to himself as a slave. "I am a debtor" is a predicate nominative. The noun debtor explains the subject. Paul's state of being, or you might say his condition, is that of being a debtor. A debtor is under obligation. Slaves are often sold into bondage because of indebtedness, so he may be capitalizing on his condition as a slave.

Why was Paul indebted to the Roman church? He didn't owe them any money and there is not a hint of Paul being indebted to them in any way, shape, fashion or form. Even so, Paul wrote "I am a debtor." A good slave who loves his master would naturally have an interest in the master's estate. The parable of the talents in Matthew 25:14ff is a good example of the slaves entrusted with the responsibility of making money for the master. Paul was a model slave and he loved not only his master, but he also loved the subjects in the master's kingdom. It was his love for his master that made him feel an obligation to all those subjects in the master's kingdom.

However, the context seems to narrow Paul's ministry in the kingdom of God. Paul said he wanted some fruit among the Gentiles. Paul's particular interest is in all non-Jewish peoples. The Greeks and Barbarians are terms that define linguistic differences among the Gentiles. However, there are cultural differences among the Gentiles. This may be a hint that the church at Rome was primarily a Gentile church. There will be other hints that it was primarily a Gentile church. The church must minister to all classes of men and women and every culture. As a personal note, are we, like the apostle Paul, debtors? What do we owe our master? We are all debtors, just like we are all slaves.

The master gives His servants gifts and those gifts are to be used for the kingdom of God. The biblical doctrine can probably best be understood from the words of Jesus Christ found in Luke 12:48: "For everyone to whom much is given, from him much will be required; and to whom much has been committed, of him they will ask all the more." Paul understood that he had an obligation to everyone, including the people at Rome. Paul's indebtedness inexorably drove him to Rome.

God not only gave the apostle Paul the best theological education available, God also gave Paul the passion and zeal to preach the gospel. The church needs men like the apostle Paul who say, "Woe is me if I do not preach the gospel" (1 Corinthians 9:16). Paul prayed that he might be able to go to Rome. His great desire was to go to Rome. Both Paul's mind and will had been prepared to preach. For that reason he wanted and planned to go to Rome to preach the gospel. The very heart of Paul's calling, his lifelong obligation, and his passion was to preach the gospel.

When Paul wrote the Ephesian church he posited: "To me, who am less than the least of all the saints, this grace was given, that I should preach among the Gentiles the unsearchable riches of Christ." John Calvin has rightly said: "When the minister executes his commission faithfully, by speaking only what God puts into his mouth, the inward power of the Holy Spirit is joined with his outward voice."

Those who hear the preaching, have an awesome responsibility. Jonathan Edwards once remarked in a sermon: "when we have heard the Word of God, we ought to give earnest heed that we don't lose what we have heard."

The preaching of the Word of God is a life and death matter. Preaching must not be considered as foolishness, because God is pleased to save people through the foolishness of preaching. It is through the preaching that justification by faith is revealed to the people of God.

3. Salvation to Everyone Who Believes

Romans 1:16-17

The theological themes and topics found in the book of Romans are deep and wide. The doctrine of the righteousness of God and justification by faith alone captured my attention throughout my Christian studies. However, they had little impact until I came to an understanding and conviction of the sinfulness of the human race. It was the concept of justification by faith alone that gripped Martin Luther the sinner and Martin Murphy the sinner. *The Westminster Shorter Catechism* describes justification.

> What is justification? An act of God's free grace, wherein he pardons all our sins, and accepts us as righteous in his sight, only for the righteousness of Christ imputed to us, and received by faith alone.

The doctrine of justification is a legal declaration and not a moral transformation. It is primarily a forensic act. Without the correct and true doctrine of justification, Christianity cannot exist. Martin Luther allegedly said, "justification by faith alone was the article upon which the church stands or falls."

There is no gospel until the righteousness of God and justification by faith alone becomes the foundation for the salvation of the fallen human race. The word "righteousness" in the Bible refers to a righteous condition or a state of being. The word "righteousness" in the New Testament always has justice in mind. Justice presupposes a moral condition. Morals describe the things that we do whether right or wrong. Righteous essentially means to be right, generally referred to in the Bible as one who is morally innocent. All men make moral decisions based on their understanding of the general nature of things. Finally, the Law of God is the determining factor of that which is right or wrong. The righteousness of God provoked Martin Luther to see his utter hopelessness and helplessness. The perfections of God make sinners aware of their sinfulness.

For some strange reason the great Princetonian divine, Dr. Charles Hodge said that the "righteousness cannot here be understood of a divine attribute." I don't see how he could say that because righteousness cannot exist apart from the righteousness of God. Righteousness does not belong to natural man after the Fall.

> Do not think in your heart, after the LORD your God has cast them out before you, saying, 'Because of my righteousness the LORD has brought me in to possess this land'; but it is because of the wickedness of these nations that the LORD is driving them out from before you. It is not because of your righteousness or the uprightness of your heart that you go in to possess their land, but because of the wickedness of these nations that the LORD your God drives them out from before you, and that He may fulfill the word, which the LORD swore to your fathers, to Abraham, Isaac, and Jacob. Therefore understand that the LORD your God is not giving you this good land to possess because of your righteousness, for you are a stiff-necked people. (Deuteronomy 9:4-6)

If human beings do not possess the essence of righteousness, then where does it come from? It comes from God. The Psalmist states it plain and clear: "He shall receive blessing from the Lord, and righteousness from the God of his salvation..." (Psalm 24:5). "I will go in the strength of the

Lord God; I will make mention of Your righteousness and Yours only" (Psalm 71:16).

Who can deny that righteousness properly belongs to God alone? It is from God's righteousness that justice prevails in the whole scheme of creation. The fundamental idea behind the biblical view of righteousness is that there is no law above God; there is no law but God's Law. The Law of God is the essence of the holiness of God. The whole book of Leviticus was given as a summary of the holiness of God. The Scripture states, "You shall therefore be holy; for I am holy" (Leviticus 11:45). Over and over again in Scripture there are numerous references to righteousness and holiness that may be summed up in the words of Jesus: "Therefore you shall be perfect, just as your Father in heaven is perfect" (Matthew 5:48).

Martin Luther's spiritual struggle began with an understanding of the righteousness of God. Luther realized his hopeless situation. God is sinless - God hates sin - man is a sinner - God punishes sin. The only hope for redemption is "the righteousness of God."

Paul devotes the first five chapters of Romans explaining, in a most profound manner, how the righteousness of God and justification by faith alone is the answer to man's hopelessness and helplessness. To put it another way, the first five chapters of the book of Romans are concerned with understanding God's promise to save His people. In chapter 1, verses 16 and 17 Paul outlines his plan for the book of Romans. In another place Paul explains, "For He made Him who knew no sin to be sin for us, that we might become the righteousness of God in Him" (2 Corinthians 5:21). The following sketch is the proposed plan of study:

> The unrighteousness of man.
> The righteousness of God leads us directly to the gospel.
> Justification is by faith alone.

17

The revelation of the righteousness of God.
The application of the righteousness of God to the unrighteous sinner.

Before we explore the righteousness of God, we must get rid of any conceit or arrogance that entertains the idea that we possess natural righteousness. We do not! We must not think that just because our Granddaddy or Daddy was a leader in the church that we deserve anything from God. We must not think that just because we've been faithful to attend church (which is a logical fallacy) that God favors us in any way. We must not think that just because we've taken the sacraments faithfully for many years that God is delighted in our faithfulness. We must not think that just because we've served as an officer in the church that God looks favorably upon our righteous service. No outward ceremonies will increase our righteousness.

Self-righteousness does not exist among the sinful human race; it is like filthy rags in the sight of God.

> But we are all like an unclean thing, and all our righteousness's are like filthy rags; We all fade as a leaf, and our iniquities, like the wind, have taken us away (Isaiah 64:6).

The prophet paints a picture of the covenant people of God, professing Christians, needing to humble themselves and ask "how can I be saved?" Whether we are wise or unwise, moral or immoral, orthodox or heterodox in our opinions, unless the righteousness of God is the ground of our acceptance before God we have no part in the salvation presented in the gospel.

So far Paul has not explained the content of the gospel. He did claim he was set apart for the good news and he served in the gospel or participated in delivering the gospel. The content of the Book of Romans majestically and in minute detail explains the gospel or the good message of salvation. If the gospel is a good message, why does Paul have the disclaimer "I am not ashamed of the gospel" or to put another way "I am not embarrassed by my testimony of the good message."

Paul asserts the gospel or good message is the power of God. This is common language for the apostle Paul. "For the message of the cross is foolishness to those who are perishing, but to us who are being saved it is the power of God" (1 Corinthians 1:18).

The words contained in the good message of the gospel are thought of as having inherent powers. It is true, "Christ died on the humiliating cross for the sins of the elect" but the words themselves are not intrinsically powerful enough to bring salvation. Many professing Christians (Pelagians and Arminians) believe that the power of salvation is in the words.

The word that should come to mind when Christians talk about God's power is *omnipotence*. Several Greek words in the New Testament are translated power. The Greek word δυναμις (pronounced *dunamis*) in Romans 1:16 is the word from which we derive the word dynamics and dynamite. The word expresses strength, ability and might. Paul's reference to the "power of the gospel" must refer to the divine strength, ability, and mightiness of God. This divine force called the power of God operates on people so that they experience a transforming power. This divine force supplies the energy for one to maintain a new way of life after the transformation from the old life. Sanctification is the term used to describe the new way of life in Jesus Christ.

The transforming power of God is also explained in Paul's letter to the Corinthian Church. "It pleased God through the foolishness of the message preached to save those who believe" (1 Corinthians 1:21). Paul's letter to the Romans and Corinthians communicate the message of the gospel; it is the gospel that reveals God's redemptive love. The power of God promises salvation for the elect and it is in this promise that unbelievers rest on Christ alone, by grace alone, by faith alone for eternal salvation. The extent of salvation is limited only to everyone who believes:

> *New American Standard* - to everyone who believes
> *New King James Version* - for everyone who believes

Paul used a present participle that emphasizes not only the initial act of believing, but the continual process of believing.

Who is able to believe? There are two classes of people described by the apostle Paul; the Jew and the Greek. Greek is a synonym for Gentile. The text does not teach the power of God unto salvation is for all Jews and Gentiles. No, it teaches that salvation is only for the ones who believe. The power of the gospel is not limited to any people at any time in human history. The power of God unto salvation is no respecter of persons. The greatest sinner as well as the most disciplined covenant child may be found by the Lord.

The Lord Jesus Christ said, "For whoever is ashamed of Me and My words, of him the Son of Man will be ashamed when He comes in His own glory, and in His Father's and of the holy angels" (Luke 9:26). Christians must not be ashamed of the gospel for it is the power of God for salvation to everyone who believes, to the Jew first and also to the Greek.

The righteousness of God is manifest to everyone who believes. The righteousness of God is the ontological theme in the book of Romans, because the righteousness of God is central to every other topic expressed in the book. There is no gospel without the righteousness of God. Likewise, faith is worthless without the righteousness of God.

The word "faith" often leaves Christians in a state of confusion. Sometimes it seems as if confusion and faith are synonymous terms to the mind of many professing Christians. For example, some professing Christians say, "just have faith in God" or "your faith will make you well" or "you need more faith."

With so much confusion about faith, Bible students must move slowly and deliberately in this discussion for a better understanding of faith relative to the Christian religion, especially biblical saving faith. For example, the word faith is used 3 times as a noun in Romans 1:17: "For in it the righteousness of God is revealed from faith to faith; as it is written, 'The just shall live by faith.'" The Greek word for faith is πιστις (pronounced, *pistis*) is a noun and is used over 225 times in the New Testament. The Greek verb equivalent to our word faith is πιστευω (pronounced, *pisteuo*) which is primarily translated "believe or trust." The Greek root for the noun and verb form is πειθω (pronounced, *peitho*) which is often translated "to persuade." Faith must have an object. Proof and persuasion accompany faith. Faith never creates anything; faith verifies what already exists. The Bible speaks of faith in things not seen. "Now faith is the substance of things hoped for, the evidence of things not seen" (Hebrews 11:1). Abraham is a good example of man who could not see the object of faith, but believed (had faith) in God's promise. There are different kinds of faith mentioned in the Bible.

> Historical faith - James 2:19 - Intellectual acceptance of truth
>
> Temporal faith - Matthew 13:20,21 - Conscience and affections stirred
>
> Miraculous faith - Matthew 8:11-13 - Faith associated with miracle
>
> Saving faith - Trust in Jesus Christ as Redeemer (*Fides Specialis*)

There are 3 elements to saving faith:

1) Knowledge (*Notitia*) - The intellectual dimension - A person must be informed about the object of faith. The person and work of Christ and His covenant promises must be made known in an intelligent fashion

2) Assent (*Assensus*) - This 2nd step in saving faith moves from gathering data to assenting to the truthfulness of the facts. Assent also includes the personal application of faith to his or her personal needs or to put it another way, recognize the gospel as the message of salvation.

3) Trust (*Fiducia*) - The volition or the will is most prominent at this point. *The Shorter Catechism* has the best language: The *Westminster Shorter Catechism* explains saving faith in simple terms.

Faith in Jesus Christ is a saving grace, whereby we receive and rest upon him alone for salvation, as he is offered to us in the gospel. The foundation of saving faith is justification by faith alone.

Paul posits, "The righteousness of God was revealed from faith to faith" (Romans 1:17). What does the Bible mean "from faith to faith?" There are various opinions from Bible scholars throughout church history.

St. Augustine: (2 opinions)
1. God's righteousness is revealed from the faith of preachers to the faith of hearers.
2. Obscure faith to clear vision.

Origen:

From faith in Old Testament to faith in New Testament.

Others:
From weak faith to strong faith (Similar to Calvin).

Calvin: As our faith makes progress and advances in knowledge, so the righteousness of God increases in us at the same time. When at first we taste the gospel, we indeed see God's smiling countenance turned towards us, but at a distance: the more the knowledge of true religion grows in us, by coming as it were nearer, we behold God's favor more clearly and more familiarly.

Charles Hodge:
"The most natural interpretation of these words is that, which makes the repetition entirely intensive, entirely of faith, in which works have no part."

If you believe with saving faith that your salvation is by Jesus Christ alone, as it is explained in the gospel, then the righteousness of God is the means of eternal life. It is the righteousness of God that secures eternal life, not faith.

Saving faith is the instrument that convinces and persuades sinners of their sin and misery. Saving faith is the instrument that gives sinners knowledge of and a desire to embrace the gospel as it is found in the Holy Scriptures.

Christians do not inherit the kingdom of God because of their saving faith. They inherit the kingdom because of the righteousness of God accounted to their souls. The unrighteous will not inherit the kingdom of God.

In an orderly and detailed fashion Christians will come to understand the Righteousness that justifies by grace through faith alone and the righteous shall live by faith. In an orderly and detailed fashion Christians will come to understand the righteousness that sanctifies by the work of God's Spirit.

4. Unrighteousness Revealed

Romans 1:18- 25

Even though the righteousness of God is the fundamental theme in the book of Romans, it is not the fundamental theme of the human race. The fundamental theme for the human race is described in great detail in Romans 1:18-3:20. The theme for the human race is the universal reign of sin. The summary of Paul's argument for this section of God's word is, "we have previously charged both Jews and Greeks that they are all under sin" (Romans 3:9).

The good man and the kinder gentler God just can't be found in this text. "For the wrath of God is revealed from heaven against all ungodliness and unrighteousness of men, who suppress the truth in unrighteousness" (Romans 1:18). Unfortunately, the wrath of God is a detestable doctrine according to most of Protestant Christianity.

How many professing Christians make "the wrath of God" the object of their study and teaching? The love of God is the centerpiece of present day Christianity. For example, the popular organization, Campus Crusade for Christ uses Four Spiritual Laws in their gospel presentation. The first spiritual law is, "God loves you and has a wonderful plan for your life." This sets the stage for a gentler kinder God. However, the emphasis in the first three chapters of Romans is the guilt of the human race. If God is righteous and just, then justice must prevail as a primary attribute of God. If God is righteous, then God must pour out His wrath on the human race. (See Genesis 2:15 and Genesis 3:1ff.)

Adam desired more than being a rational creature living in a perfect environment, so he believed the lie and became a fool. Adam the man worshipped the idol rather than the

Creator. God made the covenant and Adam broke the covenant. Breaking that covenant provoked the wrath of God. The wrath of God is an often used expression in the New Testament, but none is clearer as to the extent of the meaning of the word "wrath" as it is found in John 3:36: "He who believes in the Son has eternal life; but he who does not obey the Son shall not see life, but the wrath of God abides on him." From John 3:36 you can see that "the wrath of God" is not an emotional outburst of anger. The wrath of God is simply the punishment required because of the guilt of sin.

The little phrase "wrath of God" was a common expression used by ancient cultures. When a storm, earthquake, volcano, flood, or even an enemy invasion occurred the people cried out "the wrath of god(s)." The people thought they were being punished for their capricious evil misbehavior.

Christians must distinguish between the wrath of God and the wrath of man. God's wrath is sinless. Man's wrath is often (most often) sinful. God's wrath is his punitive justice and nothing more.

> Therefore thus says the Lord God, 'Behold, My anger and My wrath will be poured out on this place, on man and on beast and on the trees of the field and on the fruit of the ground; and it will burn and not be quenched.' (Jeremiah 7:20).

Man's wrath is an expression of cruelty, injustice and oppression. "Cursed be their anger, for it is fierce; And their wrath, for it is cruel. I will disperse them in Jacob, and scatter them in Israel (Genesis 49:7).

Man's anger is a restless and uncontrollable passion. Who are the recipients of God's wrath? Two fine Presbyterian theologians stumped their toe when they tried to explain the wrath of God. John Murray and F. Godet conclude that the wrath of God in Romans chapter 1 verse 18 is directed toward the Gentiles; their claim is without sufficient evidence. The Word of God asserts that Jews and Gentiles are guilty (Romans 3:9).

"For the wrath of God is revealed from heaven against all ungodliness and unrighteousness of men, who suppress the truth in unrighteousness" (Romans 1:18). Men is a generic term referring to all human beings including Jews and Gentiles. It is not a matter of God's anger demonstrated against human beings. It is God's wrath demonstrated against the ungodliness and unrighteousness of human beings. His wrath is poured out not upon men because they are men, but upon sin because of God's justice.

The apostle used two different words "ungodliness and unrighteousness" to describe the objects of God's wrath. Ungodliness derives from the Greek word σεβω (pronounced *sebo*) which essentially means "to worship" prefixed with the negative "a" thus not worship; therefore, ungodly.

Unrighteousness comes from the Greek word αδικος (pronounced *adikos*) which means "no righteousness." Some theologians say that ungodliness refers to a lack of reverence for God and unrighteousness refers to the moral sphere.

The manner in which men know the wrath of God is God's revelation. When something is revealed it is known empirically. God's righteousness and His wrath are known to the minds of men because God has made it known to them. The revelation of God's wrath is natural to all men because natural revelation is derived from the nature of the created world. God's wrath is a general revelation. It is general in scope and content. It is a universal principle.

We must not overlook the two little words "from heaven." The wrath of God is revealed from heaven, which means the revelation is from God. The revelation is manifest, which makes it undeniable. The wrath of God must come from God and the wrath is manifestly clear:

1. Sometimes in the form of His judgments.
2. Sometimes justice being executed by law or society.
3. Sometimes from God's Word.

God's wrath is being revealed all the time. The Greek word translated "revealed" is a present passive indicative. The grammar is definitive. It is a present tense meaning it takes place all the time. It is a passive verb so it is being revealed from a source other than the subject. It's grounded in reality. Who are the primary subjects of God's wrath? Scripture teaches His wrath comes upon those who suppress the truth in unrighteousness. To suppress means to hold back or restrain. What do ungodly immoral people suppress? Truth. The truth about what? The truth about God.

Ungodly people will always be prejudiced against the truth of God. Therefore ungodly people are prejudiced against God's nature and character, which means they are prejudiced against God's righteousness. Sometimes unrighteousness simply hates righteousness. Therefore, the truth of God is neglected by unrighteous men. Some evangelical and Reformed churches are on death row because the truth of God has been suppressed for so long.

God's people must learn to appreciate and love truth.

God's people must learn to receive and be open to truth.

God's people must develop a zeal for truth.

God's people must learn to obey God's truth.

God's people should find great comfort even though the wrath of God is being poured out in great measure, but God is sovereign and the righteous live by faith in the sovereign God.

God's revelation is so clear that it takes effort to suppress it. Men suppress the knowledge of God because it reveals the "being" of God. Rejecting the "doctrine of evidence" has become popular in the 20th century church.

Men wickedly oppose the truth of the existence of an eternal God who has revealed that He is angry with the human race. Paul the apostle concludes that all humans have some knowledge of God. The knowledge of God is not a presupposition based on anything other than self-evident knowledge. This doctrine is central to the doctrine of God's mercy and justice.

If man was/is in total ignorance of his conscionable sinfulness and in total ignorance of God's holiness, then mankind could not understand God's mercy and grace. The opposite of ignorance is knowledge. John Calvin explains, "eyes were given him (man) that he might, by looking on so beautiful a picture, be led up to the Author himself."

If man is by nature an irrational, idiotic, lunatic and beyond the possibility of knowing God, then all our evangelistic and educational efforts are a waste. However, the Bible teaches the Christian mind is renewed. God creates every human being with the capacity for reason. God creates every human being with a conscience. God creates every human being with the Law of God written on the heart.

All rational human beings have some knowledge of God; therefore, they have knowledge of God's wrath. The revelation of God's wrath is for the purpose of bringing conviction and leaving one without excuse. The revelation of God's grace and mercy is the revelation of good news to the sinner. The revelation of God's saving grace is the evangelistic message found only in the Bible.

Since all men have a certain awareness of God, they are without excuse. They cannot appear before God on judgment day and say, "but I didn't know You existed." The knowledge of God and recognizing the excellences of God's nature and character are two totally different things.

"...although they knew God, they did not glorify Him as God, nor were thankful, but became futile in their thoughts, and their foolish hearts were darkened" (Romans 1:21). They did not adore God. They were not thankful for God's providence. Even though they knew God their thoughts were useless, because they were not able to glorify God. Their minds labored, but were unable to think of that which was good. Even though they knew God, their foolish hearts were darkened.

Depraved minds are estranged from truth. Once man is estranged from the truth he moves in the direction of his own sinful inclinations.

A foolish man is an idiot of sorts; he is weak minded (Proverbs 10:8). "The tongue of the wise uses knowledge rightly, but the mouth of fools pours forth foolishness (Proverbs 15:2). Another distinguishing characteristic of a fool is: "Professing to be wise they became fools" (Romans 1:22). Why would a fool profess to be wise?

The word "fool" derives from the Greek word μωρος (pronounced *moros*). We get the English word moron from the Greek word *moros*. The definition of a moron: "A stupid person lacking in good judgment." There are several people I know whom I would consider in that class of people exactly the way the Bible describes them: "They act stupid, but they profess to be wise." The biblical text, "they became fools" is an aorist passive verb. It expresses a point in time, not necessarily past time. Emphasis is on the quality of the action rather than the time of the action.

To profess means to "assert." However, there is no evidence to follow the assertion. A person who professes something that is not real is one who pretends that something is real when it is not actually real. Unregenerate people profess wisdom and piety, but the profession is empty. They profess wisdom, but their wisdom is merely a diversion. It gave them temporary relief. Their professing wisdom was an attempt to escape from the wrath of God. They are further from the truth than someone who acknowledges that they are ignorant.

Unregenerate men become fools because God gives them what they want. Remember "became fools" is passive. They not only became fools, they changed the glory of the incorruptible God into an image made like corruptible man. Incorruptible refers to something that is not perishable. This particular action (the change) is an act of the man himself. He desires it and he does it.

It is important to understand this concept, because when man switches worship of God for the worship of something else that is called idolatry. God hates idolatry. Religious thought always has its end. The unregenerate man may not know the end, but God has an ultimate final purpose, which He reveals in the Word of God.

Paul labors to show the unrighteousness of the human race. Unregenerate people despise the true God. They divert their attention to false gods and idol worship. Idolatry leads to destruction. God lets them have their way to their own destruction. In the end the unregenerate man loves a lie more than he loves the truth. There is a real connection between a lie and an idol. The two work hand and hand. A lie, like an idol, is a mockery to reality.

The only remedy for the unrighteous sinner is justification by faith alone.

5. Evidence of Unrighteousness

Romans 1:26-32

The evidence of unrighteousness is obvious to human experience and manifestly taught in the Bible.

Rather than looking for the blessedness of God, unregenerate men seek their own ends. Every man does what is right in his own eyes (Deuteronomy 12:8). The consequence is devastating. In Paul's letter to the Romans he explains, "God gave them up to vile passions" (Romans 1:26). "God gave them up" is a form of parallelism. Paul exponentially emphasizes the immoral state of the unregenerate. Paul appears to be moving from idolatry to immorality. God reveals Himself to men, they hate God and prefer their own objects of worship, and thus the immoral unbeliever saturates himself in idolatry.

The *Wisdom of Solomon* (a book in the *Apocrypha*) posits, "For the devising of idols was the beginning of fornication, and the invention of them the corruption of life." Idolatry is the course of action that unregenerate men take that keeps them in the clutches of apostasy. Nevertheless, God gives them what they want. The unregenerate man wants liberty of choice to choose the immoral life that seems to make him happy. God gives them freedom and man must live with the consequences of his actions.

Freedom and pleasure are the haunting goals in everyday American life. Freedom is an illusion that has mistakenly duped millions of people. Pleasure is another illusion in this modern world. Pleasure requires satisfaction and no man is ever satisfied with material objects of this world. To idolize freedom and pleasure leads to immoral behavior. If we trace the history of this country over the past 100 years, we will find a society that has sought happiness from every conceivable corner. For the past 50 years this country has taken the way of the sexual revolution to discover the freedom and pleasure that seems to escape from the very grips of those who search for it.

Western civilization is very similar to the Greek/Roman culture of the time of the apostle Paul. The same sinful behavior is present today in the United States. Both civilizations commend homosexuality as an alternative lifestyle. Same sex marriage is the new normal. The Old Testament Hebrew and the New Testament Greek do not actually use the word homosexual, at least not etymologically like the English that is derived from Latin. In the Old Testament the Bible refers to sodomites and in the New Testament a sexually promiscuous man. The biblical language in Romans 1:26-28 is manifestly clear that the apostle Paul has homosexuality in mind. The church has universally accepted this passage as referring to homosexuality, until the liberals of the 20th century argued against the clear teaching of Scripture.

The early church fathers were closer to the writings of the apostles and offered historical perspective that will help the contemporary church understand the culture of that day. Clement of Alexandria was one of the earliest church fathers. He lived from 153 to around 200 A.D. In his teaching he referred to,

> The fate of the Sodomites was judgment to those who had done wrong, instruction to those who hear. The Sodomites having, through much luxury fallen into uncleanness, practicing adultery shamelessly and burning with insane love for boys.

If Christians read that statement in a contemporary newspaper, they should not be surprised at all because the ancient Greek/Roman culture and the contemporary western culture are very similar in this area. The evidence for unrighteousness is apparent in every age. This quote from St. Chrysostom reveals the unrighteousness of men:

> But nothing can there be more worthless than a man who has pandered himself (prostitutes himself). For not the soul only, but the body also of one who hath been so treated, is disgraced, and deserves to be driven out everywhere. How many hells shall be enough for such? But if thou scoffest at hearing of hell and believest not that fire, remember Sodom. For we have seen in this present life a semblance of hell."

The Dutch theologian, Herman Ridderbos, wrote:

> In this worthlessness of the inner man, this abandonment of the *nous*, as the possibility for knowing God, and in this darkening of the heart, the wrath of God is being revealed. God gives him up to the evil lusts of his heart, to a reprehensible *nous*, to do that which is not fitting. For not only is the inward man given up to darkness and ignorance in his relationship to God, but he is also perverted and inclined to all unrestraint and reprehensible activity in his moral self-determination. (*Paul: An Outline of His Theology*, by Herman Ridderbos, p. 122)

The Greek word *nous* used by Paul in Romans 1:28 requires a brief explanation. The Bible uses the Greek word *nous* to describe the condition of humanity without God (Romans 1:28). The Bible also uses a word connected with *nous* to describe the human ability to understand God by the power of the mind (Romans 1:20). The physical brain will cease to exist, but the mind will remain forever. (*Theological Terms in Layman Language*, by Martin Murphy, p. 69)

The natural condition of the human race precedes the gospel of God's saving grace. The reason many professing Christians do not make a distinction between unrighteousness and righteousness is because false teachers are not telling the truth. God may give people what they want through the mouths of false teachers.

The Word of God in 1 Kings 22:1-53 is a historical inspired event about the downfall of Ahab. The evil desires of Ahab were granted to him. It was decided in the heavenly court that false prophets, possessed by a lying spirit, would feed Ahab's ego by assuring him of victory in the battle. Micaiah's final word was "Listen all you people." These are sobering thoughts for God's people to remember because God saved them by His grace.

The capstone of Paul's argument for the universal reign of sin is stated in one verse: "And even as they did not like to retain God in their knowledge, God gave them over to a debased mind, to do those things which are not fitting" (Romans 1:28). The knowledge of God in the mind of men is the haunting punishment for the sin of idolatry.

The inescapable fact for all unregenerate humans is God must be pressed out of the mind. The late Dr. John Gerstner used Jonathan Edwards language to describe how human beings cope with the wrath of God that is ever present in their minds. The word Edwards used is diversions. Diversions are simply distractions. These diversions are the only relief available for the sinner.

The godless state of mind is always in a state of stupor, confusion, and ever contradicting itself. The insanity of the godless mind is apparent in practically every discipline of life: theological, family, education, judicial system, politics; not to mention a hodge-podge of world views communicated to the eyes and ears of infants through adulthood such as, secularism, consumerism, humanism, pragmatism, relativism, hedonism, egalitarianism, statism, et. al.

The most undesirable thought to the debased mind is God, with a big G - indisputably sovereign, all powerful, all knowing, ever present and unchangeable.

The unregenerate man may not like to retain knowledge of God, may not cherish that knowledge, but rather suppresses it. The unregenerate man does not consider God worthy of his time and attention. The certain reality that follows is evident in Paul's letter to the Romans. This refrain is the chorus that Paul sings over and over again.

Vs. 24 - "God gave them over to the lusts of their hearts"
Vs. 26 - "God gave them over to degrading passions"
Vs. 28 - "God gave them over to a debased mind"

The verb "gave" literally means "to hand over" or "to deliver up" derived from the Greek word παραδιδωμι (pronounced *paradidomi*). Luke used this word in his gospel account. "Listen carefully to what I am about to tell you: The Son of Man is going to be delivered into the hands of men" (Luke 9:44).

God gave them over to a "debased mind." Some translations use depraved mind, reprobate mind, and depraved reason. The result is God's judgment falls upon the center of the soul, which is the mind.

Seneca was a Roman philosopher who lived during the time of Jesus' earthly ministry. Although Seneca was not a Christian, he saw the prevailing unrighteousness of his day. Seneca said:

> All is full of crime and vice; there is more committed than can be healed by punishment. A monstrous prize-contest of wickedness is going on. The desire to sin increases, and shame decreases day by day. Vice is no longer practiced secretly, but in open view. Vileness gains in every street and in every breast to such an

extent that conscience has become not only rare but extinct. (*Biblical Illustrator*, Vol. 16, bk. 2, p. 110)

If Seneca could have seen Romans 1:18, he would have agreed with the "unrighteousness of men." Today many agree with Seneca but not with the apostle Paul. Morality is the object that drives man to the end of the journey of life. One thing that Seneca and Paul have in common; they believe sin is the universal condition of mankind.

Paul calls it unrighteousness. The first evidence of unrighteousness is not murder, arrogance, or insolence. The first evidence of unrighteousness is idolatry. Paul's inspired letter to the Roman Church claims idolatry is the chief sin against God. The First Commandment is "Thou shall have no other gods before me." The end of idolatry is a debased, depraved, reprobate mind, or to put in plain language, a worthless mind. Idolatry always leads to immoral behavior, social evils, and taken to its logical end, pure anarchy.

Paul introduces a list of immoral activities, which are nothing more than social evils. Paul begins this list of immoral proclivities in unregenerate humans, which are very active, "being filled with all unrighteousness.... . (Romans 1:29). It is worthy to note the participle "being filled" is in the perfect tense. It modifies the antecedent accusative object in Romans 1:28,"God gave them up. Paul posits a reprobate mind is filled with all kinds of unrighteousness.

The universal sinfulness of man is the first doctrine of Christianity relative to the fall of man. Theologians often use the term "total depravity" to describe this doctrine. The doctrine of total depravity means that every human being is a sinner in every part of his or her being, the mind, will and affections.

Unrighteousness describes the legal standing of unregenerate people before God. Unrighteousness is a broad term that encompasses a whole host of social evils. There are two other words that though similar to unrighteousness nevertheless retain their own identities. The two words are wickedness and evil. A wicked deed is essentially a bad deed. When Jesus described the false prophets He said, "every good tree bears good fruit, but a bad tree bears bad fruit." The bad condition of the heart brings the bad behavior to the open arena. His worthless mind is full of idolatry that leads to wickedness. So close are the words unrighteous, wicked, and evil, that they are hard to separate. In Acts chapter 8 Simon tried to purchase the gift of the Holy Spirit. Peter admonished Simon and said: "Repent therefore of this your wickedness (evil, maliciousness) and pray God if perhaps the thought of your heart may be forgiven." Simon's state of mind was reprobate. His mind possessed nothing but useless and worthless thoughts.

Covetousness is another word associated with "a debased mind." Covetousness refers to greed or greediness. It comes from a root word, which means "to desire to have more." Such is the reason it is interpreted covetousness. Peter uses this word in his second epistle as he describes the false prophets (2 Peter 2:3). The people described by Peter are those who hate the Word of God because it is the will of God. Furthermore they have no concern for other people. They are so self-centered they abandon any rules for intelligent and decent human discourse.

Paul reveals the evidence of unrighteousness in Romans 1:29-31. It is a vice list, or to put another way, it is a list of social evils that follow idolatry. The vice list describes the world and life view of those whom God has given over to a reprobate mind. Paul introduces the vice list as those things, "which are not fitting." These are social evils that plague every generation particularly applied to those who are not justified by faith alone.

They are full of envy. The Greek word φθονοσ (pronounced *phthonos*) translated envy is always translated envy or jealously in the New Testament. Envy is when someone sees the advantage of another and seeks to gain that advantage for himself. Paul also used the word envy in his letter to Timothy.

> If anyone teaches otherwise and does not consent to wholesome words, even the words of our Lord Jesus Christ, and to the doctrine which accords with godliness, he is proud, knowing nothing, but is obsessed with disputes and arguments over words, from which come envy, strife, reviling, evil suspicions, useless wranglings of men of corrupt minds and destitute of the truth, who suppose that godliness is a means of gain. From such withdraw yourself. (1 Timothy 6:3-5)

The context has to do with the use of wholesome or useless words. Often a man is hated because he tells the truth. The reason is the one hating him is jealous or envious of the truth teller's ability to tell the truth. A person who cannot handle reality will always envy those who by the grace of God do handle reality as it is understood in the Word of God. It is the carnal appetite that feeds on that which is false and unreal. Envy is the unbeliever's natural reaction. Dr. William Plumer said of envy:

> Envy is a malignant, restless, devilish, tormenting passion. It sickens at the worth, success or good name of others, especially neighbors. It is the great instigator of strife and of blood shedding.

Envy is particularly dangerous because it leads to murder. Obviously, taking human life is an act of treason against God, because man was created in the image of God. Murder comes in many forms. Jesus called Satan a murderer. "He was a murderer from the beginning and does not stand in the truth, because there is no truth in him" (John 8:44).

Unbelievers are full of strife. The Greek word *eris* is translated strife. In 1 Corinthians the word *eris* is translated contentions or quarrels. A striking example of what it means to be a party to strife is found in Paul's letter to the Philippians. "Some indeed preach Christ even from envy and strife, and some also from goodwill" (Philippians 1:15). The Philippian Church was full of quarrels and bitter conflict.

Unbelievers are also full of deceit. Deceit is not an outright flagrant lie. However, there are times when Paul's language makes deceit sound as if it were manifested under microscopic conditions. In early Greek philosophy, sophism was a specious argument used to deceive someone. Sophistry is a subtle false argument. To sophisticate means to mislead by deception and false arguments. To be sophisticated is actually bad, although a revised contemporary meaning is that a sophisticated person is worldly wise, mature, classy, in the know, and on top of all situations. If the root word "Sophism" is an enemy to truth, how can its derivative word "sophisticated" be good for truth? For instance, worldly wise does not necessarily express truth.

Unbelievers exhibit their unrighteousness as gossips, backbiters, slanderers, haters of God, violent, insolent, contemptuous, proud, arrogant, boasters, inventors of evil things, disobedient to parents, undiscerning, without understanding, untrustworthy, unloving, unforgiving, unmerciful, ruthless, and cruel.

The vice list describes the life of an unregenerate person. When the unregenerate person lives in and loves moral filth, there comes a point where he is given over to a reprobate mind. He may not commit all these crimes and he may commit one more than the other, but the vice list generally describes the life of a person without Christ.

Paul describes the reprobate's evil end in Romans 1:32. There is no other place in the Bible that gives such a detailed account of the unregenerate soul than Romans 1:18 - 32. The charges against him are incomprehensible. The width and depth of his sins can't be measured.

Most Christians do not like to hear about the negative character of an unbeliever. And even less, they don't like to think about the end of the unbeliever. The conduct described in Romans 1:29-31 is the conduct of the unbelieving reprobate. Paul summarizes the reprobate man as an intelligent but worthless evil worker. The unregenerate reprobate knows the righteous judgment of God. The just judgment of God is the forgotten doctrine in the modern church. However, even the reprobate man understands the just judgment of God.

The unbeliever is not destitute of the knowledge of God and God's righteous judgments. Unbelievers understand the concept of justice. Aristotle defined justice this way: "Giving a person what he is due." When the Bible speaks of justice it is inseparably tied to ethics and morality. Justice cannot exist without a moral code. Justice is one of the moral attributes of God that receives the least attention in today's church.

A just God must be a good God. A just God must also be a truthful God, because God cannot communicate to His creatures any aspect of His justice without truth. If God is good and if God is true, then He must demonstrate justice. God must give a person what is due that person. Christians may not fully understand God's justice, but they can be sure God's perfections do not allow for an error in judgment on His part.

The wicked unregenerate man knows that God's judgments are just, because God has revealed the truth to him. God has shown it to him. The unbeliever has a two edged sword to contend with:

> 1. The unregenerate unbelieving man simply rejects and suppresses the knowledge of God and adopts the material world as the object or objects of worship.

2. The unregenerate unbelieving man has no hatred of sin. Quite on the contrary he loves his sin, all the while aware that it is sin, and never thinks of repenting of it.

Unbelievers know the righteous judgment of God and they practice such things that are deserving of death. Justice requires punishment when there is a moral violation, and the punishment for violating God's Law is death.

The unbelieving reprobate is hell bound and he knows it. Furthermore he wants to take as many with him as he can. The greatest depravity of the unbeliever is his lust to encourage others to commit the crimes that are ultimately punishable to hell, unless forgiven by the Lord Jesus Christ.

It is willful deliberate rebellion against God and fellowman at the same time. To encourage someone else to sin is demonic.

> Chrysostom said: "He that praiseth the sin is far worse than even he that sins."

> John Calvin said: He, who is ashamed, is yet healable; but then such an impudence is contracted through a sinful habit, that vices, and not virtues, please us, and are approved, there is no more hope for reformation.

The redemption of a sinner is the result of God's justice demonstrated in the redemptive work of Jesus Christ. What should Christians do who live among the ungodly? Christians must be in a constant state of reformation; being reformed by the Word of God.

6. Justice in God's Judgment

Romans 2:1-3

Paul examines the noetic effect of sin from every angle and the extent of man's sinful nature. Since the phrase "noetic effect of sin" is Christian theological jargon, further explanation is necessary.

> The Greek word *nous* essentially refers to the mind, reason, or understanding. The word *noetic* comes from the Greek word *nous*. *The noetic effect of sin* refers to the mind, so the question must be asked: to what extent did the fall of man affect the mind? The *noetic* structure (the function of the mind) refers to the sum total of everything a person knows and consequently believes. For instance, Adam's ability to reason before the Fall was like the rest of creation; it was perfect. The *noetic effect of sin* did not destroy reason, but rather defaced it. (*Theological Terms in Layman Language*, p. 72)

One of the least preached and the most misunderstood doctrine of the Christian religion is man's depravity.

Sin has two effects on human beings:

1. Guilt
2. Pollution

Guilt is the obligation to punish sin and pollution is the spiritual and moral condition of the soul. The guilt of sin is the result of violating God's standard of holiness. A guilty person is accused by his Creator unless he is acquitted or condemned. Guilt can be acquitted, but pollution will remain throughout life. Paul's letter to the Romans is a prodigious theological discourse on sin, probably for 4 reasons.

1. Wicked men were reported in the church at Rome.

2. Paul wants the church informed about the universal nature of sin.

3. Leave them with a better understanding of the unrighteousness of man and the righteousness of God.

4. Justification is the only hope for sinful man.

The result of the exceeding sinfulness of the human race is condemnation. Paul posits: "you are inexcusable, O man..." (Romans 2:1). You are without excuse if you are late for school with no excuse. What happens? You are guilty; therefore, you must be punished. This principle applied to Christian theology demands God's justice. The guilt must be punished. However, God's justice cannot be satisfied with words or deeds from the mouth of an unregenerate man. The mandate applies to Jew or Gentile.

However, it may be one person whose moral constitution glows better in the public than the other, whether it was a Jew or Gentile. Some people want to act superior to others. It is the case in every age of the church. The superiority syndrome is a killer. It leads to judging the moral station of other people. It is legitimate to judge others, but the standard for judgment must be the Word of God and a right disposition in the heart.

Judging the unrighteousness of man requires spiritual insight. Jesus taught the multitude to "judge not." However, it must be taken in its context. Jesus teaches that it is wrong to concentrate attention on the little sin of another person and self-righteously criticize him without paying attention to the much greater flagrant sin in your life. Jesus condemns the Pharisees who judged others, by their own interpretation of the law, and devoted their lives on finding the sins in other people; Jesus calls them hypocrites. However, judgment is important because Jesus calls certain people dogs and swine and instructs the child of God to discriminate carefully. (See Matthew 7:1-6.)

Wickedness and hypocrisy is the result of a reprobate mind. The noetic effect of sin is evident, as John Calvin posits, "They sinned, because they were not in a right state of mind; for sin properly belongs to the mind." A worthless mind is a hypocritical mind and hypocrisy is self-condemning. People appear to be blind to their sin.

Hypocrisy may be a sub-conscious way of life for some people. They have suppressed the truth for so long they actually deceive themselves.

What we see foreshadowed in all this is the final judgment. The wrath of God will finally be poured out on the hypocrites, full and without mercy. Behind the sin of hypocrisy is idolatry. The unregenerate idolater is driven to hypocrisy because of his or her ambition to be in the place of God. Hypocrites play the part of God thus assuming the mask of one who lords it over others. Such a one is without excuse. The only hope is justification.

Paul's inspired epistle to the Romans is a witness of the sin accrued to the human race in terms of actual sin. Christians must distinguish between original sin and actual sin. The *Westminster Larger Catechism* makes the distinction.

> The sinfulness of that estate whereinto man fell, consisteth in the guilt of Adam's first sin, the want of that righteousness wherein he was created, and the corruption of his nature, whereby he is utterly indisposed, disabled, and made opposite unto all that is

spiritually good, and wholly inclined to all evil, and that continually; which is commonly called Original Sin, and from which do proceed all actual transgressions. (*Westminster Larger Catechism,* 25)

The term "original sin" can be traced to Augustine of Hippo, which he defined as "inherited sin." Although there is not a consensus on the meaning, the reformed church maintains the belief that the guilt of Adam's sin was imputed to the entire human race and it affected every aspect of the human being, mind, emotions, and will. To refine the definition of "original sin," we can say that it is the result or effect of the sin of Adam. It is that sinful condition, the absence of original righteousness, and the actual judgment on the human race.

After a scathing accusation, Paul makes a bold assertion that Christians should not overlook. Have you ever heard anybody say: "Judge not, lest you be judged?" Maybe your proof/spoof text is Romans 2:1 "in whatever you judge another you condemn yourself" but don't stop there. For what reason is one condemned who judges another? You practice the same thing. Hypocrite. Then Paul makes his bold assertion to the church at Rome: "We know." Not I hope or I guess or I suspect, but I know. The world loves a hypocrite who although he knows the judgment of God is upon him, he wants to outwardly appear as righteous. The judgment of God is according to truth and justice. Truth and justice are necessary attributes of God, because justice and truth are necessary for the holiness of God.

The Excellency of God's moral perfections are demonstrated by His justice, His truth, and His goodness. The supreme manifestation of God's truth is Holy Scripture itself. If Christians do not understand the justice of God, they will never understand the nature and character of God and therefore, they will never understand His love and His redemptive hand in creation.

Justice is God's upright character and integrity demonstrated by His correct judgment because of His Holiness. It is not possible to have justice without holiness or holiness without justice. Justice is not an easy topic. Most people really don't like the concept of justice. If they say they do, they don't know what they are saying. Jonathan Edwards said "Injustice arises from ignorance."

The righteous character of God demands absolute justice. The inspired Word of God declares the absolute justice of God (Isaiah 30:18). God's absolute justice is an ontological proposition. It reveals the pure being of God. However, God's absolute justice meets us in our creaturely nature. Christians cannot see the beginning from the end even though God is working, at this moment, to vindicate his holiness against a sinful world. God's justice is distributive in that it distributes to everyone their due. The aspect of God's justice that many cannot agree with is God's punitive justice. God must punish sin. This is Paul's message to the church.

A just God renders justice, which is his just judgment. There are several aspects to justice, one of which is the punishment for sin. All rational creatures expect to be punished for wrongdoing or what Christians call sin. "You are without excuse O man" (Romans 2:1). The laws of heathens reflect an understanding of justice as it relates to the punishment for evil works.

The law code of King Hammurabi is a good example. King Hammurabi (1750 b.c.) established laws "to establish justice in the land" (*History of Western Society*, p. 18). Hammurabi's law code called for an eye for an eye and a tooth for a tooth among equals. He favored the aristocrats over commoners and commoners over slaves, but nevertheless a primitive form of law and order. There was the element of punishment for evil in the Hammurabi law code.

One example of the Hammurabi law code: "If a physician performed a major operation on a seignior with a bronze lancet and has caused the seigniors death, or he opened up the eye-socket of a seignior and has destroyed the seignior's eye, they shall cut off his hand." There were not many doctors anxious to provide service to a dying aristocrat.

Punitive justice is God's perfection demanding that all sin will be punished.

When God was about to destroy Sodom, Abraham asked God if He would destroy the righteous with the wicked. Then Abraham said:

> Far be it from You to do such a thing as this, to slay the righteous with the wicked, so that the righteous should be as the wicked; far be it from You! Shall not the Judge of all the earth do right? (Genesis 18:25)

God is a just and impartial judge. He will always do right. God demands that all sin must be punished because God hates sin.

With the unmitigated expression of sin in Romans chapter one, Christians should expect to see the justice of God exponentially multiplying throughout the rest of the book. However, do not confuse the inaccessible distributive and commutative justice of God. Christians cannot search the depths of God's mind on the subject of justice.

To put it in a nutshell, Francis Turretin said it first and better:

> Justice demands necessarily that all sin should (must) be punished, but does not equally demand that it should be punished in the very person sinning or at such a time and in such a degree. *(Institutes of Elenctic Theology,* by Francis Turretin, vol. 1, pp. 236, 240)

The antidote for sinful man is justification by faith alone. God's justice is not capricious. Absolute eternal truth is the foundation upon which the church is able to understand God's justice. A reprobate mind, a debased mind, the mind affected by original sin cannot discern or make a right judgment. There is no justice for the creature without the intervention of God's absolute justice. The godless state of mind is always in a state of stupor, confusion, and ever contradicting itself. The insanity of the godless state is so apparent at the beginning of the 21st century. It will destroy theological integrity, family life, rational education, an uncompromising judicial system, public politics, and create many ungodly worldviews.

God's judgment comes because His justice demands it. As it has often been said "God is the perfect paymaster." He may not pay each day, week, month, or year according to His truth, but in the end He will administer just judgment.

God's judgment is according to truth. If the judgment of God is according to truth, then the fact that God is angry cannot be denied; God was angry with Miriam and Aaron because they spoke against Moses. Throughout the Bible we hear something like this:

"The anger of the Lord was kindled" (Numbers 11:10).
"They provoked him to anger" (Deuteronomy 32:16).
"They provoked Him repeatedly" (Ezekiel 8:17).

Paul sets up the wicked pervert with a no win answer (Romans 2:3). It goes something like this: It is a sin to hate God, murder, and lie, but you do those things yourself, yet at the same time you condemn others for doing them. In essence you condemn yourself. How do you expect to escape God's judgment if you can't escape your own judgment? This is an example of the ultimate hypocrite and bigot.

Even reason does not escape the judgment bar of God. The sinner's folly is to believe words will save him from the judgment of God. The essential message of the postmodernist is "my words will get me out of this mess." The postmodern unbeliever ignores the absolutism of:

> One law
> One judge
> One judgment

But this is not new; the Jews tried to escape God's judgment.

1. Their relation to Abraham.
2. Their possession of the Law.
3. Their ordinances and ceremonial feasts.
4. Their own good works.
5. The merit of their ancestors.

How do men today expect to avoid the judgment?

1. Wealth, power, position.
2. Religious association or church membership.
3. Personal morals and ethics.
4. Parents or grandparents will vindicate me.
5. Praying, giving, or doing devotions at a certain time.
6. Serving as an elder or deacon in the church.

The Jews could not avoid judgment and neither will anyone else. There is a slow but inevitable advance of Divine judgment on all of creation. The hand of God's justice will not stop until He has vindicated Himself by His acts of salvation and reprobation. The only hope is to flee to Christ and there you will find peace.

7. Revelation of God's justice

Romans 2:4-8

The Word of God makes the case clear that godless people are without excuse and godless people will certainly face the judgment.

The justice of God is a vague unspoken doctrine among evangelicals. They ask, "why is it that a man on a deserted island cannot be saved without the gospel message?" The question reveals a misunderstanding of God's justice. Professing evangelicals fail to acknowledge "the riches of God's goodness." Riches are normally associated with money and material possession, but the Bible speaks in different terms when riches are associated with God. For example, Paul writes to the Ephesians "riches of God's grace (Ephesians 1:7), "riches of God's glory" (Ephesians 1:18), and the surpassing riches of God's grace (Ephesians 2:7). The riches of God are different than material riches. God's riches are immeasurable metaphysical wealth.

God's goodness is grossly misunderstood. Paul used a Greek word in Romans 2:4, which translates goodness or kindness. The *New King James Version* uses the word goodness, while the *New American Standard Version* uses the word kindness. The Greek word κρηστοτης (pronounced *chrestotes*) referred to the notion of uprightness and Excellency. The word was used as a title of honor for rulers and dignitaries. The word in the gospel of Luke denotes excellent quality in comparison to poor quality. "And no one, after drinking old wine wishes for new; for he says, 'The old is good enough'" (Luke 5:39). You wouldn't say wine was kind enough because goodness is preferable over kindness.

Musing the unmeasured wealth of God's goodness will lead to an examination of what Scripture has to say to God's creatures about goodness. First the goodness of God comes to be known by His creatures as grace. However, when good is represented by sinful creatures, they translate it "kindness." The Bible teaches that one of the visible gifts of the Spirit is kindness (Galatians 5:22). Relative to God's justice, it is necessary to understand the difference between God's goodness and God's kindness.

The goodness of God reveals that which is good. "And we know that all things work together for good to those who love God, to those who are called according to His purpose" (Romans 8:28). The *summum bonum* (the highest good) of God's character is necessary for God's justice. God makes everything work out for good for His church.

So what do we say when people engage in evil practices? Can we say that evil is good and good is evil? Is not affliction, suffering, and injustice evil? There is a radical difference between proximate evil and ultimate good.

Martin Luther made a statement (using street language) that is apropos to understanding God's goodness. "If God told me to eat the dung from off the streets, not only would I eat it, but I would know it was good for me." Luther understood that Justice is not removed from the goodness of God. If the goodness of God cannot be separated from the justice of God, then all classes of men, including the unregenerate man, has a taste of God's goodness. "Your righteousness is like the great mountains; Your judgments are a great deep. O Lord, You preserve man and beast" (Psalm 36:6).

The elect, the true church, receives the goodness of God in a different way than the unregenerate. "Truly God is good to Israel, To such as are pure in heart" (Psalm 73:1). From God's goodness flows His love, which He communicates to His church. If God demonstrated His justice and withheld His goodness, the world would self-destruct.

The goodness of God leads to repentance most often referring to a change of mind, which is a result of God's goodness, not any human effort. The goodness of God comes to our understanding because the goodness of God is persuasive to bring us to repentance.

Unbelievers despise the goodness of God. Paul refers to "your" hardness and unrepentant heart (Romans 2:5). This is in the context of Romans 1:28 and Paul's reference to the "debased" mind or the "reprobate" mind, which is ultimately the unconverted soul; therefore, inexcusable (Romans 2:1) and despising the goodness of God (Romans 2:4). The justice of God comes face to face with the "hardness of heart."

One of the most discussed sections of the Bible on the "hardness of the heart" is found in Exodus relative to the life of Pharaoh. Ten times the Bible ascribes the hardening to God: Exodus 4:21 - 7:3 - 9:12 - 10:1,20,27 - 11:10 -14:4,8,17. Ten times the Bible ascribes the hardening as an act of Pharaoh: Exodus 7:13,14,22 - 8:15,19,32 - 9:7,34,35 - 13:15. The hardening process is the result of a reprobate heart: therefore, an unregenerate man.

This hardness of heart takes its toll on the whole soul and blindness of mind. The will is determined in opposition to God and His truth. The affections are zealous in their expression of hatred and persecution. The hard heart of an unbeliever is insensitive to the grace of God.

> This I say, therefore, and testify in the Lord, that you should no longer walk as the rest of the Gentiles walk, in the futility of their mind, having their understanding darkened, being alienated from the life of God, because of the ignorance that is in them, because of the blindness of their heart. (Ephesians 4:17-18)

Paul used two different Greek words to describe the same effect, the hardness of heart; they are ignorance and blindness.

Martin Murphy

Obviously, a hard heart cannot repent. Outwardly some form of penitence may appear to be present in the hardhearted sinner, but it is appearance only. A hardhearted person cannot be brought to repentance. There is no shame for sin and the wrath of God seems so far away. I've actually witnessed people who lie on the bed of sickness anticipating death and make verbal promises; but, when the crisis is over, so is the promise of repentance.

The hardness of heart brings about two effects: treasuring up wrath in the day of wrath and revelation of the righteous judgment of God (Romans 2:5). Treasuring up wrath in the day of wrath means the unbeliever that continues in sin will amass a great fortune, a great fortune of wrath. They despise the goodness, forbearance, and patience of God.

The unbeliever does not respond positively to the goodness of God. The righteous judgment of God is evident to the unbeliever, but he hardens himself in unbelief, pride, lust, and greed in the face of God's goodness.

The reality of God's judgment is inescapable. God's revelation in minute and absolute form describes the justice of God. The believer looks for God's goodness, forbearance and patience, but the unbeliever looks for God's wrath. The revelation of God's justice in his wrath is as sure as the day of wrath. The day of wrath is an eschatological reference to the second coming of Christ and final judgment by the Lord Jesus Christ. God will render to every man according to his deeds in the day of wrath.

> The final judgment is certain - "will render" (Romans 2:6)
> The final judgment is universal - "every man" (Romans 2:6)
> The final judgment is just - "according to their deeds" (Romans 2:6)

When God saves His elect, they are saved on the basis of the righteousness of Jesus Christ and His everlasting righteousness.

> The true church (God's redeemed people) is different than the unbelievers family of Satan.
>
> The church does not despise the Law of God.
>
> The church does not trample on the revelation of God.
>
> The church does not make mockery of God's wrath.
>
> The church is not a congregation of hypocrites.
>
> The church does not pretend to escape the judgment of God.

Unbelievers will be judged for dishonesty, slothfulness, hypocrisy, and all their evil deeds. The church will be judged for honesty, diligence, manner of worship and all those things that come from the goodness of God.

8. Justice According to the Law

Romans 2:9-13

Justice demands judgment. The Bible speaks of the final judgment in terms of God giving to each person according to what he has done. The term that is often used to describe the result of sin and final judgment is the retributive principle. The retributive principle declares the punishment suffered should correspond in degree and kind to the offense of the criminal, such as an eye for an eye, a tooth for a tooth.

Christians are explicitly included in the reference when Paul says, "For we must all appear before the judgment seat of Christ, that each one may receive what is due him for the things done while in the body, whether good or bad" (2 Corinthians 5:10).

In Christian theology the degree of punishment will be determined according to the perfect standard of God's holiness. The universality of the punishment will be "upon every soul of man." This refutes the opinion of Socinian heretics and others, who insist that the punishment of the wicked will consist in an entire annihilation both of body and soul. The terms "tribulation and anguish" signify a pain of sensation, and consequently suppose the subsistence of the subject.

The connection of punishment with sin is according to the order of Divine justice; for it is just that those who have offended the righteous God should receive the retribution for their wickedness.

Paul declared, "of the Jew first, and also of the Greek." His reference to, "the Jew first" must mean the Jew principally, and implies that the Jew is more accountable than the Gentile, and will be punished according to his superior light; for as the

Jew will have received more than the Gentile, he will also be held more culpable before the Divine tribunal, and will consequently be more severely punished. His privileges will aggravate his culpability, and increase his punishment. "You only have I known of all the families of the earth; therefore I will punish you for all your iniquities" (Amos 3:2). Although the judgment will begin with the Jew, and on him be more heavily executed, it will not terminate with him, but will be also extended to the Gentile, who will be found guilty, though not with the same aggravation. When glory and honor are promised to the Jew first, it implies that he had walked according to his superior advantages, and of course would be rewarded in proportion; while the Gentile, in his degree of revelation, would not be excluded.

Divine judgment is according to truth, therefore God's judgment is perfectly just (Romans 2:2). "For there is no partiality with God" (Romans 2:11). The truth has no respect of persons so that God's judgment will be equal to the Jew and the Gentile, so that neither the one nor the other can defend himself against the justice of God. God does not respect the master more than the servant (Ephesians 6:5-9). God does not respect the rich more than the poor (James 2:1ff). The presumption that God gives priority to one class of people more than the other class reflects the contempt for a proper understanding of God's nature and character.

The Word of God manifestly declares all human beings are inexcusable. Therefore justice must prevail. Understanding the nature and character of God is necessary for one to understand the concept of justice.

God is everything that man is not.

God is infinite, man is finite.
God is unchangeable, man is changeable.

God is all powerful, man depends on God for his power.

Man depends on God for everything including existence.

Paul argues there are two kinds of people, the Jew and the Gentile. The equality in God's judgment is based on God's Law. Sin cannot be judged and justice will not prevail unless there is an absolute, perfect, and ultimate standard.

God's Law is the perfect and ultimate standard, "For as many as have sinned without law will also perish without law" (Romans 2:12). The Gentiles didn't have the Law of God written on stones, tablets, or in a book as the Jews did. However the unbeliever was not entirely without the law for in Romans 2:15 the inspired apostle refers to the "law written in their hearts." Obviously the Gentiles have the Law of God, but not in the written form. In Romans 3:2 Paul says the oracles of God were committed to the Jews.

For the Gentiles, the Law of God found in the light of nature is sufficient to condemn even those who are not afforded the written Word of God. "Although the light of nature, and the works of creation and providence do so far manifest the goodness, wisdom, and power of God, as to leave men inexcusable…"(*Westminster Confession of Faith*, 1:1). The light of nature is abundantly bright to all men; therefore, they have to suppress the light. In biblical terms,

> the wrath of God is revealed from heaven against all ungodliness and unrighteousness of men, who suppress the truth in unrighteousness, because what may be known of God is manifest in them, for God has shown it to them (Romans 1:18).

The "unrighteousness of men" is contrary to all justice and equity.

There are logical and reasonable connections between "manifest in them" and "their conscience also bearing witness" found in Romans 2:15.

The light of nature only reveals God's anger against ungodly and unrighteous moral behavior. The light of nature does not reveal the redeeming work of Jesus Christ and therefore the light of nature will never bring salvation to the unregenerate sinner, no matter how diligently he or she might live. Those who sin without the law perish without the law. There is no salvation apart from the law of God.

"The law of the Lord is perfect, restoring the soul (*New American Standard Bible*) or as the *New King James Version* has it "converting the soul" (Psalm 19:7). God's nature is such that He demands perfection. The law is that perfection, so the law is absolutely necessary for the salvation of any human being.

The Jews had the Law, written out on tablets by the hand of God, so they have the distinct advantage, do they not? The Gentile will perish without the Law. The Jew would have been proud of Paul's statement, but then Paul says the Jew will be judged by the Law. We have to look ahead to Romans 3:23 to find out what this means to both the Gentile and the Jew: "for all have sinned and fall short of the glory of God."

God is impartial relative to Gentile or Jew. The Law determines God's decision at the final judgment. The light they have enjoyed or found unpalatable will be the ground of their judgment. Divine justice will only regard the sins of men; and wherever these are found, it will condemn the sinner. The Gentiles shall perish without Law. They are guilty; they are condemned; They shall perish.

9. Natural Law

Romans 2:14-16

"For there is no partiality with God" (Romans 2:11). God's justice is universal in its scope. It is necessary to understand the relation of the Law to God to understand the justice of God and ultimately justification by faith alone. Paul explains the universality of God's justice; "For as many as have sinned without Law will also perish without Law, and as many as have sinned in the law will be judged by the law" (Romans 2:12). Those outside the sphere of the law shall perish. The word "perish" derived from the Greek word απολυω (pronounced *apoluo*) literally means to "throw out." It refers to the ultimate fate of the wicked in this context The message to the Gentile is: You need the law to save you from the eternal expulsion from the favorable relation to the Lord God omnipotent. Those who have sinned within the sphere of the law shall be judged.

This is Paul's introduction to the universal Law of God. The law made judgment possible. The Law of God is the means by which man's moral failure can be analyzed and criticized. Justice will prevail without the written Law among the Gentiles, because they have the law in their hearts.

The Word of God explains, "for when Gentiles, who do not have the Law, by nature do the things in the Law, these, although not having the Law, are a law to themselves" (Romans 2:14). The word Gentiles in that text derives from the Greek word εθνοσ (pronounced *ethnos*) which is sometimes translated nations also refers to an ethnic group. John Calvin makes a comment on this text that must be repeated over and over again. Calvin said: "All nations. . .have some notions of justice...which The Greeks call preconceptions, and which are implanted by nature in the hearts of men."

It is important to clarify the meaning of the words "natural law" in the context of this Bible study. Natural law is so ill-defined it would take another book to bring into focus the use and misuse of the term natural law over the past 2500 years. Natural law is not natural revelation.

Natural revelation is a term used to describe general revelation. General revelation refers to the scope and content of God making Himself known. The scope is the whole world and the content is limited to natural theology. Unfortunately the term natural theology is ignored and abused by many evangelicals and the majority of conservative Reformed theologians. Natural theology refers to the knowledge rational people have of God through general revelation.

Natural law is found in early Greek philosophical thought, it is found in Christian theological expressions, and it is found among heathen writers who make no claim to clarify its definition. Natural law theories have a close relation to reason or what might be referred to as rationality. Most theologians despise natural law, because natural law is so often associated with rationalism. For instance one theologian defines it:

> Natural law in Christian theology traditionally refers to the inherent and universal structures of human existence which can be discerned by the unaided reason and which form the basis for judgments of conscience about the good and evil and which therefore make it possible to say that that right is the rational.(*Dictionary of Terms*, by Harvey Cox)

I prefer to define natural law as God's natural way of defining reality. The law I have in mind is the standard or the measure of ethics, because it tells rational human beings what they ought to do. When natural man makes a decision to act one way or the other that action reflects his morality.

The evidence for natural law is found in great abundance, apart from Scripture.

> 1. From the heathen world - Plato and Aristotle made explicit reference to natural law.

> 2. From the absurdity of no law.

> 3. From the ontological argument - Something created creation. That something was God, therefore God is in control of His creation, because dependent beings must rely on an independent being for any source of order, authority, power, and morality.

For Christians the Bible speaks loud and clear. The Law of God begins as a sound and complete system of natural laws implanted in the hearts of men. It was implanted in the heart of Adam and Eve, Cain and Abel, Noah and his sons, Abram, Joseph, and all the people even while the law of God was not written in stone. All these men of old depended on the law of God written in their hearts. Natural law was abundantly sufficient to condemn their sins and remind them of the excellent perfections of God's holiness and the need for salvation.

The concept of natural law is not an invention of recent times. However, church fathers from the first century have acknowledged natural law. A few examples from the early history of the church will suffice.

> Tertullian (160-215)- Time even the heathens observe, that, in obedience to the law of nature, they may render their own rights to the (different) ages. For their females they dispatch to their businesses from (the age

of) twelve years, but the male from two years later; decreeing puberty (to consist) in years, not in espousals or nuptials. "Housewife" one is called, albeit a virgin, and "house-father," albeit a stripling. By us not even natural laws are observed; as if the God of nature were some other than ours!

Chrysostom (344-407) - For this reason, here dismissing this subject; and having given to the laborious and studious an opportunity, by what has been said, of going over likewise the other parts of Creation; we shall now direct our discourse to another point which is itself also demonstrative of God's providence. What then is this second point? It is, that when God formed man, he implanted within him from the beginning a natural law. And what then was this natural law? He gave utterance to conscience within us; and made the knowledge of good things, and of those, which are the contrary, to be self-taught. (*Concerning the Statutes*, Homily 12. P. 421)

So where does natural law come from? It comes from God. It comes as an intuitive demonstration of man's dependency on God. Man is in a state of moral dependency from the independent being that created him. It would be out of character for that independent being to allow the dependent being to self-destruct. Otherwise the dependent being would have no purpose for existence.

Rational humans naturally know certain things about the nature and character of God. Dr. James Henley Thornwell said it best: "natural theology is that knowledge of God and of human duty which is acquired from the light of nature, or from the principles of human reason, unassisted by a supernatural revelation" (*Works of James Henley Thornwell*, vol. 1, p. 31). Rational human beings have a knowledge of human duty and moral responsibility, which is natural to them. Another 19th century philosopher posits, "If the light of Natural Theology makes us certain of anything, it assures us of these two facts, that God is a righteous ruler, and that we are transgressors." (*Practical Philosophy*, by Robert L. Dabney, p. 518)

Different translations of Romans 2:14 offer the nuances of this verse.

> *New King James Version*: "Gentiles, who do not have the law, by nature do the things in the law."

> *New American Standard Version*: "Gentiles who do not have the Law do instinctively the things of the law."

> The *New English Bible*: "When Gentiles who do not possess the law carry out its precepts by the light of nature, then, although they have no law, they are their own law, for they display the effect of the law inscribed on their hearts."

The term "nature" consists of particular characteristics, which are natural. For instance, within humanity the nature of the male is distinguished from that of the female. For some reason or the other, Christians today want to place nature and law antithetical to each other. If they mean God's Law is not natural to the human race, as God has given it to the human race, then how does man obtain an understanding of the Law? How do atheists keep the law if they do not understand it? It is clear the unbelieving world has the moral law by nature. It is so clear that Scripture says the moral law by nature is shown or proven in the lives of the Gentiles.

In Romans 2:15 the English Bible posits, "They show the work of the law written in their hearts." The English word "show" translates from the Greek ενδεικνυμι (pronounced *endeiknumi*). As a legal term it intends to inform against another party. It may also be translated "to prove." The action of the verb "show" or "prove" reflects an ongoing action and Paul's assertion reflects certainty.

Paul used the terminology "written" on their hearts, but God wrote the Law on the tablets prepared by Moses. Does the doctrine of "the Law of God is written on the heart" differ in the New Testament than the Old Testament? The word "heart" in the New Testament can refer to one of several things. It may refer to the soul of man, but the heart may also simply refer to one aspect of the soul, such as the mind or the emotions. One theologian posits, "the heart is always in Scripture the source of the instinctive feelings from which those impulses go forth which govern the exercise of the understanding and will" (*Commentary on Romans*, by Frederic L. Godet, p. 124).

God endows the souls of men with the power of reason. However, fallen human beings are still able to think and make decisions. It is not the rational inability that allows them to see their own ignorance. As Dr. John Gerstner has so well said: "It is the moral, not the natural, image which was lost in the fall" (*Rational Biblical Theology of Jonathan Edwards*, vol. 2, p 352).

The heart of unbelieving man finds the moral law distasteful. It is for that reason unbelievers hate God. John 15 speaks of those who hated God without a cause. They hate God because of his perfect moral character demonstrated by truth as the law is found in natural man.

The doctrine of the conscience comes into this discussion because the Bible teaches "the conscience bears witness on the soul" (Romans 2:15). Since the soul consists of the mind, will and emotions, the conscience must interact with the mind However, the mind and the conscience are not the same. In Paul's letter to Titus the mind and conscience are two different components of the soul. "To the pure all things are pure, but to those who are defiled and unbelieving nothing is pure; but even their mind and conscience are defiled" (Titus 1:15).

In Romans 2:15 the Gentile conscience indicates human responsibility associated with self-awareness. Although the Bible does not explicitly define the conscience, it collaborates with the soul reflected by the self-awareness of the mind and will. If there is any sense in which intuition may find a place in our being, it is here.

Notice what follows the conscience bearing witness, "their thoughts accusing or else excusing them" (Romans 2:15). The Greek word for "thoughts" is λογισμοσ (pronounced *logismos*). This word could legitimately be translated "reasonings."

Apparently, conscienceness is affected by the reasonings of the unregenerate unbeliever. Sometimes his conscience convicts him by the reasoning he employs in the process of carrying on some kind of intelligent process. Other times his conscience excuses him even when he is guilty of violating God's Law. There is a little voice inside that says what you're doing is bad. Or a little voice says, "what you're doing is good" even though in reality it is bad.

The church must boldly declare and teach the Scriptural view of natural law. Without a right understanding of natural law the devil will deceive professing Christians with the doctrine of self-righteousness. The main objection to natural law is that man is a fallen creature. Since man is a sinner he is unable in any natural sense to obey God. When an unregenerate sinner obeys the law of God he does so because of his natural ability and not his moral ability. As a result God is displeased with any obedience on the part of the unregenerate man. The Law of God written on the hearts of all men evidences itself in one of two different ways.

1) The conscience bearing witness.

2) The thoughts (reasoning) accusing or defending.

The fall did not destroy the mind; The mind was defiled, but not destroyed. The ability to function, make decisions and recognize God's law written on the heart are related to the works of the conscience.

Can the conscience err? Will the conscience always act on the side of truth? Or does the conscience concern itself with moral decisions? Since the conscience is the central self-awareness of the mind it must err in relation to truth, because it does not comprehend truth as truth, but only the obligation to do what truth requires. Likewise, the will errs in relation to choosing right and wrong, because the will only recognizes the obligation to do right. The law of God written on the hearts of all men obligates them to an absolute and ultimate authority.

Without natural law Paul could not have said and would not have said "therefore you are without excuse." Nor would Paul have considered the final judgment in the very context of this natural law discussion. Paul's arguments are inescapable;

The Jews have the Law written on tablets.

The Gentiles have the Law written on their hearts.

Whether it is the law of nature or the law of the tablets, their consciences bear witness and their reasoning powers condemn those who are without Jesus Christ.

Outward works are not a measure of how well one kept the law of God. Outward works are spurious, occasional and even they are often tainted with obvious evil intentions. External works, pomp, pageantry and proclamations will not deceive the righteous eye of God.

All men, both Jews and Gentiles, will be judged by Christ as Christ said: For not even the Father judges anyone, but He has given all judgment to the Son (John 5:22).

10. Unrighteous Jews

Romans 2:17-24

It is absolutely necessary to keep the Law perfectly for salvation. The Jews believed they actually kept the Law perfectly. It was nothing more than works salvation. All men, whether Gentiles or Jews, have the propensity to work for salvation: "the doers of the law will be justified" (Romans 2:13). The Gentiles do not have the law like the Jews have the Law, but by nature do the things of the law.

The Jews believed they were privileged people. If the Gentile who has the law of God written on the heart is without excuse, the Jew faces an exceedingly greater judgment. There is a principle in Scripture; the more revelation received means more judgment (Luke 12:48). The Jew claimed to be in a special covenant relationship with God, so by his own admission the equity of God's justice is fairly distributed upon the Jew.

One of the dangers in professing faith when there is no faith is the soul will no longer be able to stand the accusations. The law always accuses, because God is always the Judge. God is a Judge before He is a Savior.

You would expect the law of God to be a great gift, especially since the Psalmist said the law of the Lord is perfect. The problem with great gifts is that people tend to depend on the gifts. Such was the problem with the Jews. They came to rely on the law. Keeping the law, especially the ceremonial law became the test for orthodoxy; However, God warned his covenant breaking people, "I desire mercy and not sacrifice and the knowledge of God more than burnt offerings" (Hosea 6:6). God gave the Jews a gift, but they abused it.

Another advantage for the Jew was his boast in God. Boasting in God is not wrong, but if the boast is from pride and arrogance it is a sinful boast. Another advantage for the Jew was he claimed to know God's will. Since the Jew had the Word of God, he had the advantage of testing anything in life to see if it was right or wrong. The advantages for the Jew are substantial, but none more significant than, "being instructed out of the Law" (Romans 2:18). To put it another way it literally means being instructed by Word of mouth. God actually speaks to His people. God's gifts are honorable and worthy for a very special people.

The Jew also has advantages in his relation to the rest of the world. The Jews were self-righteous theonomists. "Also He [Jesus] spoke this parable to some who trusted in themselves that they were righteous, and despised others" (Luke 18:9). They were confident that they were guides to the blind. No doubt, the light given to the Jew was superior to the natural law written on the heart of the Gentile.

The Jews considered themselves to be a light to those who were in darkness. The responsibility of the Jew in relation to the Law is clearly expressed in terms of "an instructor of the foolish, a teacher of babes, having the form of knowledge and truth in the law" (Romans 2:20).

The Jew may not have been more mature than the Gentile, but the Jew had the meat of the Word as an instrument to bring him to maturity. The Jew had a distinct advantage over the Gentile in every way, but none more glaring than "the embodiment of knowledge and truth." The Jew didn't see his understanding of knowledge and truth as competing with other world religions and philosophies. The Jew had the advantages of having the Law given directly from the mouth of God.

The Jews were privileged people, but as is often the case people take advantage of special privileges. The Jew had a distinct advantage over the Gentile in every way, because he had the form of knowledge and truth in the law written on the tablets of stone. If the Jew had so many advantages and privileges over the Gentile, it logically follows the Jew would live an exemplary life. As the apostle Paul has said:

The Jews were instructed in the Law.

The Jews were confident of their estate.

The Jews were able to teach the less fortunate.

Paul didn't say it, but he alluded to the central truth that more knowledge and understanding means more responsibility. Paul's letter to the Jews in the church at Rome must have hit hard.

If you bear the name of a Jew.

If you know God's will.

If you are instructed from the Law.

If you are a guide to the blind.

If you have the embodiment of the knowledge and truth.

The Jew had a treasure in the Law, but the treasure had to be used the right way. The Jews bragged about their having the law, but Jesus warned them of their shortcomings.

"You have heard that the ancients were told, 'You shall not commit murder' and 'Whoever commits murder shall be liable to the court'" (Matthew 5:21).

"But I say to you that everyone who is angry with his brother shall be guilty before the court; and whoever shall say to his brother, 'Raca,' shall be guilty before the supreme court; and whoever shall say, 'You fool,' shall be guilty enough to go into the fiery hell." (Matthew 5:22)

"You have heard that it was said, 'You shall not commit adultery.'" (Matthew 5:27)

"But I say to you, that everyone who looks on a woman to lust for her has committed adultery with her already in his heart." (Matthew 5:28)

"Again, you have heard that the ancients were told, 'You shall not make false vows, but shall fulfill your vows to the Lord.'" (Matthew 5:33)

"But I say to you, make no oath at all, either by heaven, for it is the throne of God." (Matthew 5:34)

The Jews, like all sinful human beings, want to play games with truth. The unregenerate wicked deceiver will often make more of an effort to distort the truth than the regenerate believer will to protect the truth. However, believers who are in different stages of sanctification will distort the truth to a greater or lesser degree. Like the Jew who believed that you have to actually commit adultery to break the 7th commandment is a good example. Many people do not violate the 7th commandment if it is understood literally yet such an interpretation is superfluous. Paul's rhetorical questions fly in the face of those who brag about their knowledge and understanding of truth.

You, therefore, who teach another, do you not teach yourself? You who preach that a man should not steal, do you steal? You who say, "Do not commit adultery," do you commit adultery? You who abhor idols, do you rob temples? You who make your boast in the Law, do you dishonor God through breaking the Law? (Romans 2:21-22)

The Jews were teachers of the Law as is explicitly stated in the New Testament, but the question is: what did they teach? They taught tradition and hypocrisy. And the Pharisees and the scribes asked Him, "Why do Your disciples not walk according to the tradition of the elders, but eat their bread with impure hands" (Mark 7:5)?

Then Jesus spoke to the multitudes and to His disciples,

The scribes and the Pharisees have seated themselves in the chair of Moses therefore all that they tell you, do and observe, but do not do according to their deeds; for they say things, and do not do them (Matthew 23:1-3).

The fundamental question was, "do you ever teach yourself anything?" To put it another way, "Since you know the truth, do you apply it to your life?" Paul's next rhetorical question cuts to the core: "The one preaching do not steal, do you steal?" As one theologian has said, "Theft comprehends all the injustices and deceptions which the Jews allowed in their own commercial affairs." Honesty in business dealings is one of the most abused of all the commandments. It is easy to teach the 8th commandment, but living by it is a different matter. As the English scholar Dr. Leon Morris has said, "It is easy to preach honesty to other people, but not nearly so easy to be scrupulously honest in all one's own dealings. We are always tempted to grade honesties." I expected Paul's next question: "The one who says not to commit adultery, do you commit adultery?" Sexual perversion was a serious problem in Rome at the time Paul wrote this letter, even among Christians. It is a serious problem today. Paul chose theft and adultery as representative questions from the second table of the Law.

Paul's next question moves us to the 1st table of the Law: "The one detesting idols, do you rob temples?" Theft comes into play again, but the emphasis is on idolatry. From the readings in the Talmud, it would appear that some Jews profited by promoting idol worship although, they themselves did not engage in idol worship.

Paul finally sums up the condition of the Jew. The great advantage for the Jew was the Law, so to break the Law was to dishonor God. God must have the highest place of honor. To dishonor God is to dishonor the profession of faith. The Puritans called this experiential religion. To blaspheme God's name is to defame his name. Experiential describes personal experiences, past and present. Jonathan Edwards explains:

> This is properly Christian experience, wherein the saints have opportunity to see, by actual experience and trial whether they have a heart to do the will of God and to forsake other things for Christ, or no…so is that properly called experimental religion, which brings religious affections and intentions, to the like test. (*Works of Jonathan Edwards*, vol. 2, *Religious Affections*, Yale ed., p. 452)

It means God's people have the wrong attitude toward God. The Law will not give you the right attitude toward God, but it will show you the nature and character of God.

It will show you your total and absolute inability to meet God's holy standards. Therefore, God's people need to be justified by faith, because they cannot perfectly keep God's Law.

11. Sacramental Salvation

Romans 2:25-29

Pride is a chief sin among those who think they are privileged. The name of God is often cursed because religious people are hypocrites. The Jews bragged about their importance because God had shown favor to them throughout history.

Since Judah survived the fall of 10 northern tribes in 722 B.C., it was the tribe of Judah that was expected to return to Jerusalem and re-establish the temple and worship.

> Thus says the Lord of hosts 'In those days then men from every language of the nations shall grasp the sleeve of a Jewish man, saying, Let us go with you, for we have heard that God is with you.' (Zechariah 8:23)

Although the Jew had the special privilege of having the written Word of God, the Jew was a sinner just like the Gentile. Therefore, the Jew was under condemnation just like the Gentile. However, Paul gets in the face of the Jews accusing them of pride, arrogance, and self-righteousness. The Jews believed in sacramental salvation. Paul warned the Jews of their error. You think you are special because you have the written Law, but you think you are even more special because you are marked with circumcision (Romans 2:25). Circumcision was the formal act of being admitted in the covenant community, which is equal to joining the church through covenant baptism. However, the Jews made circumcision a saving sacrament.

Martin Murphy

And God said to Abraham: "As for you, you shall keep My covenant, you and your descendants after you throughout their generations. This is My covenant, which you shall keep, between Me and you and your descendants after you: Every male child among you shall be circumcised; and you shall be circumcised in the flesh of your foreskins, and it shall be a sign of the covenant between Me and you. He who is eight days old among you shall be circumcised, every male child in your generations, he who is born in your house or bought with money from any foreigner who is not your descendant. He who is born in your house and he who is bought with your money must be circumcised, and My covenant shall be in your flesh for an everlasting covenant. And the uncircumcised male child, who is not circumcised in the flesh of his foreskin, that person shall be cut off from his people; he has broken My covenant." (Genesis 17:9-14)

After 1900 years of covenant breaking the Jews had come to trust the act of circumcision as the sacred act that produced eternal life. Rabbi Menachem said in his commentary: "Our Rabbins (masters) have said that no circumcised man will see hell." Rabbi Levi taught, "In the hereafter Abraham will sit at the entrance to Gehenna and permit no circumcised Israelite to descend therein"

What the act of circumcision meant to the Jews, baptism means for many professing Christians. They believe baptism secures salvation. Paul understood circumcision was the sign by which the Jew was admitted into the covenant, but circumcision was only profitable if the Law was kept. "For circumcision is indeed profitable if you keep the law; but if you are a breaker of the Law, your circumcision has become uncircumcision" (Romans 2:25).

80

Perfect obedience was required by the individual Jew to bring about salvation. Keep in mind he is addressing the Jews at this point. Can any man keep the Law perfectly? Did Paul mean that by "doing the law" that the covenant member must respond to the law of God with a sincere, genuine, heartfelt love of obedience that results in fruitful Law keeping? The apostle was certain that no one is justified by doing the works of the law. "Therefore by the deeds of the Law no flesh will be justified in His sight, for by the Law is the knowledge of sin" (Romans 3:20).

Joining the church through the sacrament of baptism is of no use unless there is evidence that God has changed the heart. The external act does not guarantee an internal change. Paul's irony in Romans 2:26 must not be taken literally. It may be an inference to natural law. "Therefore, if an uncircumcised man keeps the righteous requirements of the Law, will not his uncircumcision be counted as circumcision?" The Gentiles were not in a covenant relationship with God; therefore, they only had the law written on the heart, natural law. Paul is thinking ahead to the latter part of Romans chapter 3 and chapter 4 where he will deal specifically and judiciously with justification by faith. What I think he intends in verse 26 is to make a hypothetical statement to show that salvation depends on obedience, in this case the obedience of Christ, for salvation. Paul wants to cut off any thought that circumcision or any good deed is the ground or basis for justification. Paul challenges the pride and arrogance of the Jew who thought he was favored by God just because of the external mark of circumcision.

Paul challenged the confidence of those Jews who did not understand their standing before God. "And will not the physically uncircumcised, if he fulfills the Law, judge you who, even with your written code and circumcision, are a transgressor of the Law" (Romans 2:27)?

The contemporary church is no different in principle than the Jewish church underage 2000 years ago. It is easy for professing Christians who are unbelievers to take pride in sacramental salvation. Sacramental salvation is the same in principle as works salvation. It is merely self-salvation. Psychology refers to it as the ego. Pauline theology used terms like "old man" and "flesh" to describe the unconverted soul. The Bible describes this condition:

> For you have trusted in your wickedness; You have said, 'No one sees me'; Your wisdom and your knowledge have warped you; And you have said in your heart, 'I am, and there is no one else besides me.' (Isaiah 47:10)

God may have given professing Christians exceptional abilities to understand the Word of God or the ability to learn the system of doctrine taught in Scripture, but they are still sinners.

The true Jew is one who has the inward change.

> For he is not a Jew who is one outwardly, nor is circumcision that which is outward in the flesh; but he is a Jew who is one inwardly; and circumcision is that of the heart, in the Spirit, not in the letter; whose praise is not from men but from God. (Romans 2:28-29)

How does this inward change take place? Not by being called a Jew. Not by being circumcised. Moses explains:

> The Lord your God will circumcise your heart and the heart of your descendants, to love the Lord your God with all your heart and with all your soul that you may live. (Deuteronomy. 30:6)

The theocratic covenant national identity of Israel was not sufficient to insure a right standing with God and a place in His eternal kingdom. Neither is membership in a church enough to buy a place in Heaven. Paul intends to convey the truth that external things serve the purpose of signification by symbolism. The inner spiritual reality of a relationship with God is the only assurance of a right relationship with God. Religion is a passion in the lives of most people. Often there is no fruit of the spirit, but there is a deep and abiding passion for religious activity.

Justification by faith alone must precede any necessary and good works.

12. God's Judgment is Just

Romans 3:1-8

Paul's inspired words to the church at Rome concludes in chapter two with the charge to Gentiles and Jews that they stand before God inexcusable. Chapter 3 is like the proverbial final nail in the coffin. Finally and fully Paul explains that all men are sinners. Paul's literary style often reminds me of a symphony. The crescendo will eventually fill the room with its powerful full harmonious music. Paul's message to the church of all ages is not hard to digest, but it may be unpalatable to the senses of rational beings.

All men are sinners.

Justification is by faith.

Although Paul was concerned about the souls of his Jewish brethren, Paul lays two charges before the Jews:

1) the law (privileges)

2) circumcision (covenant benefits)

After Paul shows how the Jews are blessed with the law and circumcision, he throws two rhetorical questions at their feet.

What is the advantage of being a Jew?

What is the benefit of circumcision?

The words "advantage" and "benefit" require brief comments. The word "advantage" derives from the Greek word περισσοσ (pronounced *perissos*) and may be translated over and above, abound, having more than enough, and beyond the regular size. The Greek word *perissos* refers to that which surrounds a thing, but it is not a part of it. The English word "benefit" comes from a Greek word that may very well be translated "profit" or "value."

It is evident from the New Testament that the Jews considered themselves pre-eminent in that ancient world. They thought they were preferred above all others; Jews were privileged people. They were privileged because they were entrusted with the oracles of God. The oracles of God simply referred to divine utterances given to the writers of Holy Scripture. In the ancient world the Greek word for oracles was used among the unbelievers to denote their pagan gods and later was applied to their shrines. Paul's reference to the oracles of God is nothing more than the Word of God written.

The Word of God was a great advantage, a privilege for the Jews. It was a moral advantage because the Word of God gave them the Law of God. The Word of God also gave them the promises of God. God's threats and promises are absolutely truthful. However, God's threats of wrath and promises of salvation do not come like we might expect them.

The Word of God is the absolute truth and source of all wisdom, because it comes from the mouth of God. The Word of God is unique in that it speaks to the hearts of men, professing Christian believers and unbelievers. (See 2 Corinthians 2:12-17.) When wicked men hear the Word of God fear falls upon their souls. When wicked men hear the Word of God their conscience is pierced. When godly men hear the Word of God, they find joy and comfort. When godly men hear the Word of God they find support and assurance. Truth will always reveal the distinction between the believer and the unbeliever.

The war cry of the World Council of Churches back in the middle of the 20th century was "doctrine divides, service unites." The heathen world is inclined to turn the creation of heavens and earth into idols. The oracles of God have the necessary elements for a sound civil government. God's general providence allows for the government of nations, but it is from Holy Scripture you find ethical standards that regulate economic, social, and political relationships. The Bible calls for men to be generous with God's provision and to promote wholesome laws, foster fair dealings and promote peace and liberty.

The Word of God provides the church with a literary volume that reveals the fullness of truth. Unfortunately, the Word of God is read and not comprehended even among many whom call themselves serious inquirers. The fallen intellect will have conflicting theories of truth without the Spirit of God.

The Word of God informs the church that justification by faith opens the door for works of service. That is why Paul said the Jews had the advantage in every way, because God gave them His word. "For everyone to whom much is given, from him much will be required; and to whom much has been committed, of him they will ask the more" (Luke 12:48). God is true, but every man that does not believe the Word of God is a liar. "Let God be true" is a fundamental maxim of all Christian philosophy.

Although professing Christians still have the sinful nature, they experience outward blessings and privileges. Sometimes those blessings and privileges are replaced with self-conceit and self-righteousness. Professing Christians, like the Jews, have a great advantage by having the Word of God. They must not ignore God's Word.

Professing Christians have a great profit by having the sacraments to fill them with God's grace. What a tragedy to abuse this marvelous means of grace. It appears the contemporary church does not see the difference between the covenant keeping holy God and the covenant breaking sinful man.

Then was it wrong for God to punish Judas Iscariot? Was it wrong for God to punish the Jews? Is it wrong when God punishes anyone for sin? No, God is a just God. God will punish no one more than they deserve. God's vengeance is always righteous. God's justification is a demonstration of God's righteousness. Paul explains:

> But if our unrighteousness demonstrates the righteousness of God, what shall we say? Is God unjust who inflicts wrath? (I speak as a man.) Certainly not! For then how will God judge the world? For if the truth of God has increased through my lie to His glory, why am I also still judged as a sinner? And why not say, "Let us do evil that good may come"?—as we are slanderously reported and as some affirm that we say. Their condemnation is just. (Romans 3:5-8)

It is true that the sin (unrighteousness) of men will bring glory to God. There is yet another possibility we may consider from Paul's question. The question may very well be a reference to the theological use of the Law. Others might say, "if our unfaithfulness makes no difference to God's faithfulness, what point is there for us in being faithful." This applies to antinomianism that teaches, "sin as you please."

Paul seems to anticipate the questions being thrown at him by the congregation at Rome. There are three possibilities to consider:

1) How will God judge the world (a future action)?
2) If God doesn't judge the Jews, how can he judge the Gentiles?
3) If God is unjust, how can he judge the world?

verse 5 - Is God unjust?
Verses 6 - Absolutely not

The word "truth" in verse 7 corresponds to the word "righteous" in verse 5. The word "lie" in verse 7 corresponds to the word "unrighteousness" in verse 7. You can easily see the Hebrew parallelism in verses 5 and 7.

Verse 5 - But if our lie demonstrates the truth of God.
Verse 7 - For if the righteousness of God has increased through my unrighteousness.

If God is glorified when I tell a lie, why would God judge me? Answer: The judgment of my sin reveals the perfections of God. One theologian explains:

> Suppose the truth of God, in his predictions, promises, or denunciations, should be more abundantly manifested to his glory, by any man's telling a willful lie: why should the liar be punished for giving occasion to the display of God's glory? The answer is that our want of right motives, our evil intentions and our violation of the law forbidding all falsehood are the ground of condemnation. The good brought out of moral evil by the overruling providence of God, and the result have nothing to do in estimating the heinousness of sin. So says the human conscience. So says God. (*Commentary on Romans*, William S. Plumer, pg. 114)

Now why has Paul gone through this eloquent rhetoric? Paul wants the church to understand God's judgment is just. Sin does not produce good, sin produces sin. God will be glorified, but the sinner stands condemned. God is righteous when He punishes them for their sin.

13. The Power of Sin

Romans 3:9-20

The apostle Paul has argued from every angle to prove all men are sinners.

1. All men are sinners because of the fall.

2. Gentiles know they are sinners because they have the Law of God written on their hearts.

3. Jews know they are sinners because they have the written Word of God.

Paul's final appeal to the truth of his grand explanation is from the Word of God; "they are all under sin" (Romans 3:9). *Harmartilogical* doctrine is the study and application of sin. The biblical doctrine of sin is inseparable from the doctrine of justification. Jonathan Edwards posits, "sin is self-love without God."

Sin has been redefined in the postmodern world. Today sin is an action taken that is perceived to damage the environment. Sin is merely the bad example of good people. Sin has two dimensions, which may be described as original and actual. Sin is universal as a result of original sin; Therefore, sin affects every aspect of creation.

The apostle moved carefully but deliberately in his letter to the Romans to bring them to this very critical juncture. Paul asserted that the Jews had an advantage over the Gentiles. Then Paul asked a rhetorical question: "are the Jews any better than the Gentiles?" Paul's answer is a resounding no!

The Jews had the advantage of having the Word of God, but the Jews stand before God the same as the Gentile, a condemned sinner. Are the Jews any better off than the Gentiles? Paul said, "No we have previously charged that they [Jews and Greeks] are all under sin." The word "charged" appears to be a legal term used in court to accuse someone of a crime. This Greek word is only used here in the New Testament and cannot be found in any other early Greek writing. Many scholars believe the word originated from the Greek word αιτια (pronounced *aitia*) which is a legal term used frequently in the New Testament as well as in other early Greek writings.

For instance, In the Papyri we find a letter with this comment: "he was sent to Alexandria to meet a charge against him and make his defense; but since he did not succeed in clearing himself he is forcibly detained." The fact that someone was charged with a crime does not make it so. I wonder why Paul used this language rather than "We have proved." The *King James Version* used the word "proof" rather than the *New American Standard* and *New King James Version*, which used the word "charged." To charge is to accuse.

The apostle Paul used these same words in various texts that deal with the subject of sin. "I am carnal, sold under sin" (Romans 7:14). "All men are under sin" or to put it another way all men are bad which is contrary to God's goodness (Galatians 3:22).

Theologically speaking, it is not just the fact that men are under the power of sin, but more to the point is the truth that mankind loves to sin. Adam's transgression sealed all men under sin and ultimately death.

The authority of the Law is universal; therefore, the Law speaks to everyone under the Law. The Law not only speaks universally with authority, but speaks with power. The Law will close every mouth. The Law is convincing, therefore, the Law convinces one of condemnation and death.

No one, except Jesus Christ, can fulfill the Law and that is the reason men are shown how weak they are. If they recognize they are unable to fulfill the Law in their own strength, then every mouth may be stopped. Their inability, their lack of power, and their lack of authority over moral considerations drive them to humility or diversions.

God will not permit the attitude taken by King Nebuchadnezzar: "I am and there is no one else besides me" (Isaiah 47:10). If a man thinks himself great, that man will be stopped by the law of God. As John Calvin says, "Let all be little ones, and let all the world be guilty before God" (*Institutes of the Christian Religion* 2.7.9, by John Calvin). Calvin understood as we all should understand that the only way to close every mouth to pride and arrogance is man must be able to escape condemnation.

> For so long as a man has anything, however small, to say in his own defense, so long he deducts somewhat from the glory of God. Thus we are taught in Ezekiel how much we glorify his name by acknowledging our iniquity: "Then shall ye remember your ways and all your doings, wherein ye have been defiled; and ye shall loathe yourselves in your own sight, for all your evils that ye have committed. And ye shall know that I am the Lord, when I have wrought with you for my name's sake, not according to your wicked ways, nor according to your corrupt doings" (Ezekiel 20:43, 44). If part of the true knowledge of God consists in being oppressed by a consciousness of our own iniquity, and in recognizing him as doing good to those who are unworthy of it, why do we attempt, to our great injury, to steal from the Lord even one particle of the praise of unmerited kindness? In like manner, when Jeremiah

exclaims, "Let not the wise man glory in his wisdom, neither let the mighty man glory in his might, let not the rich man glory in his riches: but let him that glorieth glory" in the Lord, (Jeremiah 9:23, 24,) does he not intimate, that the glory of the Lord is infringed when man glories in himself? (*Institutes of the Christian Religion* 3.13.1, by John Calvin)

The Law of God will allow no human being to excuse himself nor work his way into heaven. "Whatever the law says it speaks to those who are under the Law, that. . .all the world may become guilty before God" (Romans 3:19). This is what we call original sin. All men are under the guilt of sin. It means that there is the liability for punishment.

Standing before God is not a good place to be if His Law is the judge. Paul explains: "Therefore by the deeds of the Law no flesh will be justified in His sight, for by the Law is the knowledge of sin (Romans 3:20). Knowledge of sin comes from the knowledge of the Law.

> The Law demands entire, perpetual and absolute obedience and every man has knowledge of his short comings.
>
> The Law accuses human beings of foundational sins, such as pride, lust, and covetousness.
>
> The Law accuses men of sins of ignorance. The more light the more Law; and the more Law, the more conviction.
>
> The Law accuses men of secret sins and corrupt thoughts.
>
> The Law accuses men of sins of omission.

The Law accuses men who are in rebellion even when they know they have sinned.

The Law occupies one place for a universally sinful human race to convince and to condemn.

So why do men keep the Law? They keep the Law with the expectation of earning some merit with God, and unhappily so because they think that God will find some pleasure with their law keeping. Relative to the doctrine of justification by faith alone, the works of the law are ultimately unfulfilling to man and totally unworthy before God.

The works of the Law for unconverted man are wasted works because they will not remove the judgment. No man can be justified by keeping the Law. Self-justification is an impossible notion.

Before unconverted people can be ready for the gospel, they must be convinced of sin and humbled by its condemning power. The demands of the law are so great that they must have a power other than their own, a power that can meet the requirements of the Law

14. Justified by Faith Alone

Romans 3:21-31

Paul devoted every bit of energy he could muster to prove that all men, women, boys, and girls are sinners in the sight of God; therefore, they are guilty before God. Having been condemned by the Law we now come to the saving work of Jesus Christ. Jesus Christ is the center piece of Paul's whole display of God's holiness and man's sinfulness.

Jesus Christ is the most talked about figure in human history. The *Encyclopedia Britannica* uses 20,000 words to describe Jesus Christ. Jewish historians write about Jesus who is called the Christ. Men of prominence and learning have always admired Jesus Christ and have even attempted to model themselves after their understanding of Christ. Even liberal theologians attest Jesus Christ as the model of morality and ethics.

Jesus Christ, the God-man, is a mystery indeed. We can't say enough about Him. As the Apostle John said, "There are many things that Jesus did, which if they were written one by one, I suppose that even the world itself could not contain the books that would be written" (John 21:25).

Reflect on the prophet preeminent who reveals to His people by His Spirit and the Word the whole will of God. Reflect on Jesus Christ the priest whose sacrifice is without blemish and is continually making intercession for Christians. Reflect on Jesus Christ the King who rules over Christians and defends them against the enemy.

The gospel is empty without the God-man, the Lord Jesus Christ, as He is explained in the gospel of John. Christ is the central figure in the doctrine of salvation. If Christ represents

His people, His people must understand the person and nature of Christ.

The God who created the world and all the wealth in it came to live in abject poverty. He was born in a borrowed manager. He slept in borrowed beds. He borrowed a boat to preach from. He was buried in a borrowed tomb. Jesus Christ was the light of revelation to the Gentiles and the glory of God's people Israel.

Salvation, redemption, forgiveness of sins, the atonement, regeneration, and justification cannot exist without Jesus Christ. As Paul says in Colossians 2:15, "Jesus Christ is the image of the invisible God."

The teaching of two German theologians of the 19th century began the process of reducing Jesus Christ from God to man. The first one was Friedrich Schleiermacher. He concluded that Christ was a new creation in which human nature was elevated to the plane of ideal perfection. Schleiermacher, more than any other man in recent history, made man the object of devotion rather than God. To Albrecht Ritschl, Christ was a mere man, but nevertheless the supreme moral works of Christ earned Him a place in the Godhead. Ritschl ruled out the pre-existence, incarnation and virgin birth of Christ. The teaching of Schleiermacher and Ritschl have multiplied a 1000 times over. Liberalism and pietism are enemies of Christ and His church.

Jesus Christ is the Savior and Lord of His church. In order to be the Savior of the church, Christ had to satisfy God's justice, which is nothing less than perfect Law keeping.

The book of Romans explains in great detail how and for whom Christ satisfied God's justice. The theme is justification, but many related aspects must come into play. Justification is one dimension of God's saving action. God's saving action begins with regeneration, which renews the state of the soul. Then the soul is altered by God's act of justification.

Justification is the 3rd logical step in the logical chain of salvation:
1st - Effectual calling or regeneration
2nd - Repentance and faith
3rd - Justification
4th - Adoption
5th - Sanctification
6th - Glorification

Martin Luther taught that God's act of justification is the article by which the church stands or falls. The *Westminster Shorter Catechism* answers the question, What is justification? Answer: "An act of God's free grace, wherein he pardons all our sins, and accepts us as righteous in his sight, only for the righteousness of Christ imputed to us, and received by faith."

The church must take great care to preserve the doctrine of justification by faith alone. The essence of the doctrine is found in the Book of Romans.

But now the righteousness of God apart from the Law is revealed, being witnessed by the Law and the Prophets, even the righteousness of God, through faith in Jesus Christ, to all and on all who believe. For there is no difference; for all have sinned and fall short of the glory of God, being justified freely by His grace through the redemption that is in Christ Jesus, whom God set forth as a propitiation by His blood, through faith, to demonstrate His righteousness, because in His forbearance God had passed over the sins that were previously committed, to demonstrate at the present time His righteousness, that He might be just and the justifier of the one who has faith in Jesus. (Romans 3:21-26)

The revelation of God's righteousness is the necessary doctrine preceding the doctrine of justification by faith alone. Righteousness has to do with a person's standing before God. Paul began his letter to the Romans by bringing the revelation of the righteousness of God before them. The manifestation or the revelation (making something known) of God's righteousness is necessary to understand how a person is related to God. The dilemma is stated in Romans 3:23.

The certainty that every person has sinned.

Every person continually falls short of God's standard of righteousness.

What is the answer to man's dilemma and God's wrath? Jesus Christ paid the price for the sins of His people, those whom He chose before the foundation of the world. Jesus Christ is the redeemer. Christians should not take redemption for granted, but Christians should take redemption as a guarantee.

Jesus Christ is the Christian's propitiation. The use of the word propitiation in general terms is a technical word used in the Old Testament referring to the "Mercy Seat." It describes the covering of sins by the High Priest each year.

The word propitiation (in verb or noun form) is used in the New Testament in the sense of forgiveness, mercy, and grace. The Greek word ιλαστηριοσ (pronounced *hilasterios*) found in Romans 3:25 is translated propitiation in the *New King James Version* and the *New American Standard Version*.

The word propitiation is used many ways in the Old Testament.

Genesis 32:20 - Jacob wanted to appease Esau.

Exodus 32:30 - Moses wants to make atonement for sins of the people.

2 Chronicles 30:18 - Hezekiah prays for the Lord to pardon.

Propitiation is a sacrifice that appeases God who hates sin and is radically opposed to it. The dilemma between God and man is that finite man has nothing to offer the infinite God. The solution was to offer an infinite sacrifice, the Person of Jesus Christ.

Jesus Christ as a human suffered pain, joy, feelings, et al. God sent His Son, the person of Jesus Christ to be the propitiation for the sins of His people. The sacrifice of Jesus Christ required the spilling of His Blood to satisfy the wrath of God. The relationship between Him and His blood was important to the Old Testament church as well as the New Testament church because life and blood are closely related. God displayed Jesus Christ "as a propitiation in His blood through faith" (Romans 3:25).

Professing Christians profess their faith in other people, a preacher, their job, or even themselves. The biblical mandate is to live a life of faith with full assurance that Christ became a sacrifice so believers could express their faith.

God in His sovereignty gave His church a propitiation, which was well pleasing and acceptable in His sight. The Bible speaks clearly about the relation of propitiation to justification. "For we maintain that a man is justified by faith apart from works of the Law" (Romans 3:28). "Therefore having been justified by faith, we have peace with God through our Lord Jesus Christ" (Romans 5:1). "The Law has become our tutor to lead us to Christ, that we may be justified by faith" (Galatians 3:24). "Nevertheless knowing that a man is not justified by the works of the Law but through faith in Christ Jesus, even we have believed in Christ Jesus that we may be justified by faith in Christ, and not by the works of the Law; since by the works of the Law shall no flesh be justified" (Galatians 2:16).

Justification is an act of God secured because Jesus Christ satisfied God's divine wrath against His elect. Justification springs from the fountain of God's grace (Titus 3:4-5).

Justification *makes* no one righteous, neither is it the bestowment of righteousness as such, but rather it *declares* one to be justified whom God sees as perfected once and forever in His beloved Son. The guilty sinner is not *made* righteous. The guilty sinner is *declared* righteous.

Throughout the history of this doctrine the principal point of difference and dispute has been whether faith is the only condition of justification or whether good works in connection with faith are also to be regarded as an instrumental cause. Opinion has run to opposite extremes from Protestant antinomianism to the Roman Catholic doctrine of penance and works of supererogation. The term, "supererogation" used in Roman Catholic doctrine explains one may receive more merit than is needed to enter into heaven. The extra merit goes into the treasury of merit. Christ plus the saints are said to have more merit than they need, so the surplus merit goes into the treasury of merit, to be distributed to others. A Roman view of substitutionary atonement wherein the substitute is not only Jesus Christ, but other men with more merit that they need for themselves to enter heaven.

A chief cause of error has been an undue magnifying of the intellectual element in faith at the expense of the element that is moral and practical. Even in the earliest days of Christianity the tendency was to regard faith as merely a mental assent to Christian doctrine. The possessor of such faith deemed himself as having fully met the gospel requirement, though regardless of the claims of Christian service and even of ordinary morality.

Thus the scriptural doctrine of justification by faith became, to a considerable extent, beclouded in the early period of church history. Abuses later became prevalent in the Roman Catholic Church through the failure to maintain the clear teaching in Scripture.

From the Canons of the Council of Trent, Chapter VII: "In What the Justification of the Sinner Consists, and What are its Causes?"

> The efficient cause of justification is the merciful God who washes and sanctifies gratuitously. The instrumental cause is the sacrament of baptism, which is the sacrament of faith, without which no man was ever justified. The charity of God is poured forth by the Holy Ghost in the hearts of those who are justified . . . all these infused at the same time, namely faith, hope and charity.

> Canon 9 of the Council of Trent:

> If anyone says that the sinner is justified by faith alone, meaning that nothing else is required to co-operate in order to obtain the grace of justification. . .let him be anathema.

> Canon 11 of the Council of Trent:

> If anyone says that men are justified either by the sole imputation of the justice of Christ . . . to the exclusion of the grace and the charity which is poured forth in their hearts. .let him be anathema.

In his final declaratory statement Pope Pius IV said this:

"I likewise profess that in the Mass a true, proper, and propitiatory sacrifice is offered to God on behalf of the living and the dead . . ."

You may be thinking that was 450 years ago. The Roman Catholic Church published a catechism in 1995. Their views on justification have not changed.

1989 - Justification is not only the remission of sins, but also the sanctification and renewal of the interior man.

1991 - With justification, faith, hope, and charity are poured into our hearts, and obedience to the divine will is granted to us.

1992 - Justification is conferred in baptism. Justification conforms us to the righteousness of God, who makes us inwardly just by the power of his mercy. Pause and think of the problem; what happens if someone sins after baptism? The Sacrament of Penance is necessary to restore the sinner to God's good favor.

Chapter XVI, Canon 29 of the Council of Trent:

If anyone says that he who has fallen after baptism cannot by the grace of God rise again, or that he can indeed recover again the lost justice but by faith alone without the sacrament of penance... let him be anathema.

The biblical doctrine has not changed. Paul's rhetorical question is an eye opener. "Where is boasting then? It is excluded. By what law? Of works? No, but by the law of faith" (Romans 3:27). The Jews trusted in their own works of the law. The desire to keep the law for the sake of earning salvation dismisses any reason to desire justification by faith. Boasting has no place in God's plan of salvation.

It doesn't matter if you call it self-esteem or self-glorification, if you see the ground of acceptance in your own merit, then you have not been justified by faith alone.

15. Justification Doctrine in the Old Testament

Romans 4:1-16

"Those whom God effectually calls he also freely justifies" (*Westminster Confession of Faith, ll.6*).

Effectual calling refers to the biblical doctrine of regeneration.

> But you are a chosen generation, a royal priesthood, a holy nation, His own special people, that you may proclaim the praises of Him who called you out of darkness into His marvelous light..."(1Peter 2:9)

Regeneration is the radical and complete change of the soul by the power of the Holy Spirit of God. The regenerate soul is described as a new creation. In plain language it refers to the birth or beginning of a new creation. The mind, will, and emotions turn from self to God. The mind will then discern spiritual truth and spiritual reality. The will is enslaved to Jesus Christ, so that obedience to Christ becomes pleasure and joy.

Although Christians have been effectually called by the power of God with an enabled soul, they still have the problem of guilt. Although God has given Christians a new soul, the soul is still guilty and must be punished.

Christians may find relief by believing and understanding the biblical doctrine of justification. It is an act of God's free grace. Consider the analogy of a man who is in debt to another. The debtor then has a third party freely and without any strings attached to pay the debt. The third party had to meet the obligations required to pay the debt, so it was not freedom on his part because he was compelled to meet the requirements of the lender. Justification is God's gracious act whereby God acts freely within the covenant of grace to accept in the sinners place, the perfect work of Jesus Christ.

Paul devoted a substantial portion of his letter to the Romans explaining Abraham's justification. There are at least two reasons for Paul's interest in Abraham's justification.

> 1.   Abraham was called the father of the Israelites. "And Jacob said, O God of my father Abraham, and God of my father Isaac." Abraham was also recognized in the New Testament. "Your father Abraham rejoiced to see my day: and he saw it, and was glad" (John 8:56). The Old Testament Jews had practically canonized Abraham.

> 2. Abraham was the first of God's covenant people to use the language that defines justification by faith (Genesis 15:6).

Justification is not just a New Testament doctrine, because Abraham lived around 2000 B. C. The term justification is essential to understand the salvation of the church. It is absurd to think that God had no interest in the salvation of the Old Testament saints. Paul did not want to set aside the Old Testament teaching and since Abraham was noted as a man who was justified in the Old Testament, Paul uses Abraham in presenting the doctrine of justification to the church at Rome.

If Paul can establish Abraham as the object of God's grace and Abraham was justified by faith, Paul can establish the necessity of the doctrine of justification to the church at Rome.

Then there may be yet a third reason that Paul brings Abraham into the picture. Paul previously made an assertion that he will have to defend. Paul will have to answer the question: Are Christians justified by faith or are they justified by works (Romans 3:28)? If man can earn his justification, then he has a reason to boast. Paul said, "if Abraham was justified by works, he has something to boast about, but not before God" (Romans 4:2).

Compare Paul/James and use of words justification, faith and works. (See Paul/James Controversy, page 153)

The depth with which Paul inquiries into the doctrine of justification should get the attention of the church. If the Bible says something one time that one time is sufficient to establish its truth. But when the Bible refers to a doctrine over and over in Scripture in both the Old Testament and New Testament, it deserves careful attention.

Why is the doctrine of justification so important? There are many reasons, but the fundamental doctrine is the irreparable dichotomy between the holy God and the sinful man. To put it another way God is an absolutely sovereign just judge and man is an unredeemable criminal.

Worship, morality, creation, or anything else is worthy of attention, but none of those things bring comfort to a guilty soul. In legal terminology guilt refers to the condition one stands before the court. To put it another way after all the evidence is in, it is then proven that the criminal broke the law and deserves the due punishment.

The scene in the heavenly court is the irreparable dichotomy between God and man. What are the two possible solutions for the criminal?

1) He can plead for the court to show mercy and not punish him according to his crime.

2) He can work to pay his crime debt.

In human law courts there are some crimes that could be worked out. For example, a man steals $100, then works for the person and pays back the $100. In God's court the crime is of such nature that man cannot pay the debt, so the death penalty is the punishment. Justification by faith alone is the central doctrine of salvation. That is the reason Paul quoted Genesis 15:6, "Abraham believed God and it was accounted to him for righteousness." Abraham believed the inception of his faith finds its culmination in God accounting or declaring Abraham a righteous man.

Abraham's faith is not limited to a certain period of time. It was sufficient so that God declared Abraham a righteous man. God declared Abraham righteous on the basis of the sacrifice of Christ. Theologians describe God's declaration of righteousness in terms of:

Propitiation - satisfaction of God's divine wrath.

Expiation - Removal of guilt of original sin.

The central Protestant doctrine of justification teaches that sinful man is *declared* righteous in the sight of God.

The Roman Catholic Church was afraid of the doctrine of justification by faith alone. They argued that the sinner is not actually justified. Justification that does not *make* a man righteous is nothing more than deception. The Roman Catholic Church posits the act of justification must be accomplished by infused grace. Justification must be actual and not forensic.

Roman theologians say they smell antinomianism in justification by faith alone. Are they right? What about Dispensationalism? In his critique of Dispensationalism, Dr. John Gerstner has a chapter entitled "Dispensational Antinomianism the Antithesis of True Grace, Part One." Dr. Gerstner explains the historic dispute about *meritorious* works and *necessary* works. Dr. Gerstner wrote, "From the essential truth that no sinner in himself can merit salvation, the antinomian draws the erroneous conclusion that good works need not even accompany faith in the saint" (*Wrongly Dividing the Word of Truth*, by John Gerstner, Second ed., p. 241).

Rome was rightfully concerned that some loose gun in the Protestant Church would twist Scripture and corrupt the doctrine of justification. Rome countered this potential problem by teaching that justification must be *actus physicus*, an "actual physical" act. The Protestants responded: justification is *actus forensio*. Justification is the "actualization of a legal condition by an act of God."

The debate never ended, but Luther left the church with his famous response "*simul justus et peccator*" - at once righteous and a sinner. Justification happens while believers are still sinners.

Rome's view is that justification is accomplished by the actual infusion of grace into the soul. Again Luther responds with "*justitia alienum*." The Latin term *Justitia* refers to righteousness. *Alienum* means alien, which is a foreigner.

I agree with Luther, Calvin and many of the other reformers, but more importantly I believe the Bible. "Abraham believed God and it was accounted to him for righteousness" (Genesis 15:6).

The clear teaching of the Bible is denied if the church tries to attach meritorious works to the doctrine of justification. "Therefore by the deeds of the law no flesh will be justified in His sight" (Romans 3:20). "For if Abraham was justified by works, he has something to boast about, but not before God" (Romans 4:3).

Is it possible to exercise our faith? No! Paul says, "For by grace you have been saved through faith and that not of yourselves; it is the gift of God, not of works, lest anyone should boast" (Ephesians 2:8). Christians often say, "I exercised my faith" implying a meritorious work.

The English scholar, Dr. Alister McGrath, wrote a book on the history of the Christian doctrine of justification. In that book Dr. McGrath said:

> Who Christ is becomes known in his saving action; who man is, becomes known through his being the object of that saving action. The doctrine of justification thus encapsulates the essence of the Christian faith and proclamation, locating the essence of Christianity in the saving action of God towards mankind in Jesus Christ. (*Iustitia Dei: A History of the Christian Doctrine of Justification*, Third Edition, p. 2)

Paul's whole argument is that Law and grace are not equally substantial causes of our salvation. The cause of our salvation is not good works.

Christians are regenerated, justified, and adopted into the family of God. Without justification and a proper understanding of it, professing Christians are not in the family of God. "For the promise that he would be the heir of the world was not to Abraham or to his seed through the law, but through the righteousness of faith" (Romans 4:13).

When Paul said, "the promise was not to Abraham through the law, the apostle simply means that faith was independent of law keeping. Abraham also understood that his faith was independent of circumcision. The sacraments are received by the faithful, they don't produce faith. They are aids to increase our faith, but the sacraments cannot produce faith.

The Roman Catholic Church never sorted out the correct biblical doctrine of justification by faith because they teach the sacraments actually produce faith. They wouldn't say so in so many words, but their own dogma demands it.

> Born with a fallen human nature and tainted by original sin, children also have need of the new birth

Baptism to be freed from the power of darkness and brought into the realm of the freedom of the children of God, to which all men are called. (*Catechism of the Catholic Church*, Second Edition, 2016, p. 319)

Medieval scholasticism clearly taught that the sacraments convey grace to the recipients unless there is some other spiritual roadblock. The Roman Catholic Church used the Latin phrase *ex opere operato* (by the work performed) therefore it was operative grace.

The Reformed theologian Francis Turretin carefully followed the teaching of Scripture.

Our opinion is that the sacraments do not work grace physically and *ex opera operato* as if they possessed a force implanted and inherent in them of conferring and effecting grace; but only morally and hyper physically, inasmuch as they are signs and seals which in their lawful use hold forth and seal grace to believers (God by the power of the Holy Spirit truly performing and fulfilling in them whatever he promises and figures by the signs). (*Institutes of Elenctic Theology*, by Francis Turrretin, vol. 3, p. 363)

The Protestants have always rejected the effacious power of the sacraments. Paul's conclusion is based on the Word of God.

Therefore it is of faith that it might be according to grace, so that the promise might be sure to all the seed, not only to those who are of the Law, but also to those who are of the faith of Abraham, who is the father of us all as it is written, "I have made you a father of many nations" in the presence of Him whom he believed—God, who gives life to the dead and calls those things which do not exist as though they did. (Romans 4:16-17)

For the Jews, they must forget tradition and the volumes of interpretive redactions, and consult the Word of God to understand how they stand before God.

For the Gentiles, they must turn to the Word of God as the final source of authority for their understanding of the promise, faith and grace. Jews and Gentiles are justified by faith alone.

16 Hope in Faith

Romans 4:18-25

The reformed theologian, Francis Turretin quotes *The Council of Trent*, Canon 8 to show the violent reaction of the Roman Catholic Church against justification by faith alone:

> If any man shall say that grace is not conferred by the sacraments of the new law themselves *ex opera operate*, but that faith alone in the divine promise is sufficient to obtain grace; let him be accursed (*Institutes of Elenctic Theology*, vol. 3, p. 362, by Francis Turretin).

The Protestants have always rejected the effacious power of the sacraments.

Paul's relentless pursuit to expound the doctrine by which the church stands or falls continues in the later verses of Romans chapter four. The entire doctrine of justification by faith alone is necessary for forgiveness of original sin and all actual sins. Abraham was a man that understood forgiveness. Christians should understand forgiveness all the more because of the abundance of God's grace in this dispensation. Abraham's faith was important for Abraham himself as well as God's people who lived during the time of Abraham. The doctrine of justification by faith alone was not for Abraham alone, but for all children of God. Christians are informed, strengthened, and edified by the doctrine. This is an important aspect of the remnant.

However, all people are not the objects of God's justifying grace. Who are the objects of God's justifying grace? The answer is those, "who believe in Him who raised up Jesus our

Lord from the dead" (Romans 4:24). This requires close thinking. Who are "those who believe?" The Word of God shows the difference between "professing" Christians and "actual" Christians. Professing Christians are those who profess to be Christians, but do not believe or act like Christians.

> They went out from us, but they were not really of us; for if they had been of us, they would have remained with us; but they went out, in order that it might be shown that they all are not of us. (1 John 2:19)

> I know that after my departure savage wolves will come in among you, not sparing the flock; and from among your own selves men will arise, speaking perverse things, to draw away the disciples after them. (Acts 20:29-30)

> Not everyone who says to Me, 'Lord, Lord,' will enter the kingdom of heaven; but he who does the will of My Father who is in heaven. "Many will say to Me on that day, 'Lord, Lord, did we not prophesy in Your name, and in Your name cast out demons, and in Your name perform many miracles?' "And then I will declare to them, 'I never knew you; depart from Me, you who practice lawlessness.' (Matthew 7:21-23)

Those who are born by the Spirit of God and justified by faith alone certainly have a right relationship with God. That does not necessarily mean that everybody who says "I believe" actually has a right and favorable relationship with God. To believe means to have faith. In reference to true (actual) believers Paul said, "who, contrary to hope, in hope believed" (Romans 4:18).

The word "hope" as it was used by Paul, does not fit the description of the word hope in contemporary language. Most people probably think of the word hope meaning some optimistic and fortunate future. For example someone may say, "I hope taxes don't go up next year." Biblical hope is very different. Biblical hope is grounded in God's promises. Hope and faith are often intermingled in the Bible. Another example of faith and hope from a biblical perspective is found in Paul's letter to the Colossians.

> He has now reconciled you in His fleshly body through death, in order to present you before Him holy and blameless and beyond reproach if indeed you continue in the faith firmly established and steadfast, and not moved away from the hope of the gospel that you have heard, which was proclaimed in all creation under heaven, and of which I, Paul, was made a minister. (Colossians 1:22-23)

Paul said Abraham "in hope believed." What was the object of Abraham's hope? That he would father a child. If you think you've experienced a hopeless situation, let's review Abraham's hope against hope. First, Abraham "contemplated his own body, now as good as dead, since he was about 100 years old." Granted there may be men who have enough reproductive ability to produce a child at 100 years of age. I've never met one and would expect if that possibility were a reality that it would be rare indeed. So let's grant that Abraham was a rare man. Does that mean that he should hope for a child at his age? That depends on the woman. If he was 100 and the woman was 25, it is possible. However, Abraham's wife had a problem. The Bible says she had a dead womb. The Greek word for "dead" is νεκροσ (pronounced *necros*). Dead is the opposite of alive. It was not possible for Abraham and Sarah to have a child by the power of their flesh.

If those are the kind of circumstances that you've encountered, then you had a hopeless situation unless God intervened. Now if God promised to intervene and you believe the promise of God, then you would have every reason to hope against hope. The weakness of the flesh is a real problem. The crux of the matter is frustration of not knowing how to sustain life. Paul has already said: "God gives life to the dead and calls into being that which does not exist" (Romans 4:17). Talking about insecurity, we're all insecure if we depend on the flesh for anything of a permanent nature. This is the message we find in Hannah's prayer in 1 Samuel 2:

The Lord kills and makes alive.

He brings down to the grave and brings up.

The Lord makes poor and makes rich.

In the face of the weakness of the flesh, Abraham continued to hope against hope. The promise of justification is not just to Abraham it is to "those who believe."

When Christians are challenged by the trickery of men and the craftiness of deceitful scheming, the temptation to deny that which they have learned from Scripture or anything that threatens their assurance, they should hold tightly to this portion of God's Word.

If Christians believe, they must guard against any unbelief. Abraham "did not waver in unbelief" (Romans 4:20, NASV). The word "waver" is an interesting word. The *King James Version* translates it he, "staggered not through unbelief." The Greek word διακρινω (pronounced *diakrino*) translated waver or stagger essentially refers to someone using their own judgment and reason in discerning between one thing or another. An example of staggering in unbelief is found in Elijah's challenge at Mount Carmel.

So Ahab sent for all the children of Israel, and gathered the prophets together on Mount Carmel. And Elijah came to all the people, and said, "How long will you falter between two opinions? If the Lord is God, follow Him; but if Baal, follow him." But the people answered him not a word. Then Elijah said to the people, "I alone am left a prophet of the Lord; but Baal's prophets are four hundred and fifty men. Therefore let them give us two bulls; and let them choose one bull for themselves, cut it in pieces, and lay it on the wood, but put no fire under it; and I will prepare the other bull, and lay it on the wood, but put no fire under it. Then you call on the name of your gods, and I will call on the name of the Lord; and the God who answers by fire, He is God." (1 Kings 18:20-24)

God has given the church His precious promises to stand in the face of the temptation of unbelief. Abraham was strengthened in his faith. God took a weak Abraham and gave him strength. Abraham's strength did not come from his rational willing ability. Abraham's strength came from God and not from Abraham's faith. Faith can't produce anything. You can believe until your brain dries up, but your belief will not create anything.

You believe because the Holy Spirit gave you new life in Jesus Christ. When the Holy Spirit changes your heart you will believe that Christ was delivered up for your sins and Christ was raised so you would have confident hope in your justification.

17. Justification, Peace, and Love

Romans 5:1-5

Justification is the catalyst, which seals our reconciliation to God. When a person is reconciled to God that person becomes a new creature. Reconciliation to God naturally and necessarily leads to reconciliation with God's people. Reconciliation is one of the many benefits of justification and justification is an integral aspect of the Christian's covenant relationship with God. The fundamental premise of justification is that it establishes and is the foundation upon which a human being is related to God in a saving way.

Paul describes the unique relationship that God has with His children. "Therefore, having been justified by faith, we have peace with God through our Lord Jesus Christ" (Romans 5:1). A few grammatical comments are necessary because the relationship of justification and peace is so crucial. "Having been justified" is a participle. The participle modifies or in some way associates with some other noun or verb in the sentence. Participles are useful and necessary to express an idea. One Greek scholar has said: "In them [participles] lurk hidden meanings and delicate shades of thought that intensify and clarify the thought of the sentence" (*A Manuel Grammar of the Greek New Testament*, by Dana & Mantey, p. 258) The participle "having been justified" is aorist referring to a onetime event and passive, which means it happened to you. In this text it is an act of God. The participle "having been justified" modifies "we have" which is a present tense verb. It may be stated this way: "what you have now and continually have is the result of a previous action." The grammar is important. It reflects the unique relationship of God's judicial act to the human experience.

Justification is necessary to have peace with God. The Hebrew and Greek word for peace is widely translated in English in different nuances such as friend, favorable, greet, health, prosperity, perfect, safe, secure, and well-being. Peace is opposite to war. If there is peace, there cannot be persecution, temptation, condemnation, alarm, strife, contention, and contradiction. The condition we call peace is the condition that everyone wants, but very few seek peace.

Peace is a condition that accompanies the biblical doctrine of Love. "If someone says, 'I love God,' and hates his brother, he is a liar; for the one who does not love his brother whom he has seen, cannot love God whom he has not seen" (1 John 4:20). John has a way with words. Some of his words appear hyperbolic, others must be interpreted analogous to faith, and then some are literal.

John's language is worthy of consideration. "If someone says 'I love God'" it is a conditional phrase in the Greek text, which assumes man does not love God. In the text someone does not *say* he hates his brother, rather he hates his brother. It shows the inability to love.

The familial language communicates to the average person. John's use of the word "brother" in this context must refer to a child of God that is God's representative. Loving God's representative may not be easy, but God commands it. Love one another. John's inspired word tells us that to hate one of God's children is the same thing as hating God. It is very possible to profess to love God and indulge in hatred toward a child of God, but the condition repudiates the profession. Hatred implies war and the opposite of war is peace, so man cannot hate a brother and have peace with God at the same time.

The language in John's epistle must square with the rest of Scripture. Justified sinners have the capacity to hate and lie; therefore, they also have the capacity be out of fellowship with God and they may also be out of fellowship with man.

Although Christians desire peace and it is a condition that brings joy, happiness, and optimism, peace does not give them a right standing with God. Only justification can give a right standing with God.

The prophet Isaiah said: "There is no peace" says the Lord "for the wicked." Imaginary peace is no peace at all. Christians have real peace because they are justified. They have a Mediator who is the prophet, priest, and king.

Peace with God is, no doubt, the greatest benefit of justification by faith, but it is not the only benefit. There are benefits attached to justification that will never be fully realized by most professing Christians in their life time.

Paul said, "we have access by faith into this grace in which we stand." Admission into a state of God's grace means God's favor is a permanent aspect of the state of salvation. The word "standing" is connected with the imagery of a court. For example, what is the posture when one appears before a king? Standing or kneeling? Which is best? If one stands it is because the king has favored that person. Everyone wants to stand in the presence of the royal court with the approval of the king. If the king approves of us we should then stand firm on the hope of his promise for future favor. Our state of grace is fixed by the giver of the gift.

The second benefit of justification mentioned by Paul is that we rejoice in the hope of the glory of God. Hope is not frivolous speculation. Hoping in the glory of God is a profound comfort to God's people because they are confident of the promised peace from God whose glory is ever present.

The third benefit of justification is found in Romans chapter 5 verse 3. "We glory in tribulations." The *New King James* translators may have used the word "glory" to give the appearance of godliness to what might otherwise be considered a sinful response to tribulations. The Greek word καυχαομαι (pronounced *kauchaomai*) literally means "to boast" or "to have pride in." Obviously, godly people must not be prideful, for pride is a deadly sin. Paul used the word "boast" most often and in fact it is not found in the gospels, or other New Testament writers. Paul does not mean Christians should boast in their tribulations. Paul later said, "For I consider that the sufferings of this present time are not worthy to be compared with the glory that is to be revealed to us" (Romans 8:18). We are not proud of our tribulations. Our tribulations should weigh heavily not because we are such great soldiers, but because we know that God uses them for our benefit and for His kingdom.

Given the context of Romans 5:3, is it possible to have peace and tribulation at the same time? The word "tribulation" is often connected with persecution and suffering for the sake of the Kingdom of God. "For indeed when we were with you, we kept telling you in advance that we were going to suffer affliction; and so it came to pass, as you know" (1 Thessalonians 3:4). Jesus said, "Blessed are you when men cast insults at you, and persecute you, and say all kinds of evil against you falsely, on account of Me" (Matthew 5:11). Christians should guard against the pressure of giving in when they are under pressure. When Christians suffer affliction it may be a means of sanctification.

Justification is an act, but it is an act that has an ongoing effect. Paul explains:

> We also glory in tribulations, knowing that tribulation produces perseverance; and perseverance, character; and character, hope. Now hope does not disappoint, because the love of God has been poured out in our hearts by the Holy Spirit who was given to us (Romans 5:3-5).

The domino effect moves into every part of the Christian experience. If affliction comes from the grace of justification, Christians are all set to a resolution that requires patient endurance. Patience is listed in Galatians 5:22 as a fruit of the Spirit. Paul says that patient endurance produces character. The word "character" needs some explanation. The Greek text refers to the process or result of a trial. I'm reminded of the ordeal used to test the innocence or guilt of a party. Proven character is nothing more than our experience from the trials and afflictions as Christians.

The aged Christian who has received the benefits of justification through the years by his or her suffering and affliction will be greatly blessed in apprehending an understanding of God's covenant promises. Christians need experience to be effective in their calling.

God does not tell us to believe a smickildilly unless we have some knowledge of the smickildilly. We often confirm what God has promised by some experience with the smickildilly. There are times when experience is the best teacher Christians can have, especially if they experience suffering for the sake of the gospel.

Our Christian experience naturally leads to hope. Hope is a certain assurance. For that reason Paul says that hope does not disappoint. Hope that remains constant and sure will not disappoint.

The benefits of justification ultimately reflect the love of God. Theologians have debated what the "love of God" means in this text for nearly 2000 years. God's love to us assures us of His mighty presence, but our love of God demonstrates our hope in His covenant promises.

God loves us and for that reason we receive the benefits of justification by faith alone.

18. Christ Died for Those Justified by Faith Alone

Romans 5:6-8

The most wicked act of rebellion known to mankind was the greatest blessings ever known to mankind. Christians don't normally think of death bringing joy, happiness and blessing. The reality of death is a blessing for those who are justified by faith alone, but a curse to the unbeliever.

> For when we were still without strength, in due time Christ died for the ungodly. For scarcely for a righteous man will one die; yet perhaps for a good man someone would even dare to die. But God demonstrates His own love toward us, in that while we were still sinners, Christ died for us. (Romans 5:6-8)

The evangelical church certainly teaches the death of Christ on the cross, but I fear for the wrong reasons. I think selfishness and pietism are the main reasons evangelicals speak scantily on the subject. Sometimes people die for causes that they deem right, but even then it is a selfish motive.

People die for those whom they love. Many life giving sacrifices are associated with emotional passionate moments. But at the weakest point the sacrifice is for "the good" as Paul says. People do not die for those whom they hate.

Are we righteous or good? The question to ponder, "what is the difference between a righteous man and a good man?" The righteous man is the man who keeps the whole Law. The good man must be a better man because Paul says that one might die for a good man.

The good man not only keeps the whole Law, but also in order to be good he must be generous to his fellow man. He must love the one for whom he dies. With all the love a human can muster, maybe one would die for a good man.

Martyrdom is often associated with the spirit of patriotism and doing good, but once it is complete it is forgotten. The only martyrdom that is not forgotten is that which accomplishes its purpose. But the question is: which one of us is righteous and which one of us is good?

Paul has two concepts in mind. Justification is a theological term meaning the righteous man is justified. *Summum bonum* is a Latin phrase referring to the highest good, the supreme good. It is a philosophical term that provides the ethical concept by which all others are measured.

Religiously or philosophically, there is no righteousness apart from an external work that we cannot claim as our own. Who has reached the highest level of morality to which everyone else should aspire?

The answer is simple. He sent His Son, the Lord Jesus Christ to die for His people, the righteous and the good. God loves the elect sinner. If love is to be understood in the biblical sense, we should note that sacrifice is the true test of love. Christ became a sacrifice to those who were not only sinners, but also His enemies. This is the primary teaching of Christianity. "For I delivered to you first of all that which I also received; that Christ died for our sins..." (1 Corinthians 15:3). For a guilty condemned sinner the first in importance is that Christ died so the guilt might be removed.

The discriminating truth of Christianity is the death of Jesus Christ procured the salvation of God's people. Jesus Christ was punished. The elect were redeemed. God's redemptive love is arbitrary. God's justice is absolute. God loves because of who He is and not what any creature has done. There is nothing lovely about sinners, yet God loves them and Christ died for them.

One of the profoundest few words in the English language is "We have peace with God." Peace with God is a state of being. The nearest explanation I have as to why God justified me, gave me peace, and poured His love into my heart is that I couldn't justify myself, I could not acquire peace as a condition, and I am incapable of producing love apart from the Spirit of God. The Word of God explains in these terms:

> NKJV - when we were still without strength
> NAS - while we were still helpless
> NIV - when we were still powerless
> RSV - while we were still weak"

Although each translation has a difference nuance, the translation comes from the Greek word meaning "strength" prefixed with a negative; therefore, "no strength" or "without strength." The idea that man is without strength might imply that he was only weak, but still alive. The Greek word explains the condition of man before regeneration and justification.

> Unredeemed men are helpless (Romans 5:6)
> Unredeemed helpless men are ungodly (Romans 5:6)
> Unredeemed ungodly men are sinners (Romans 5:8)
> Unredeemed sinners are enemies of God (Romans 5:10)

This is the moral inability Jonathan Edwards talks about. Dr. Gerstner explains moral inability in *Rational Biblical Theology*: "Moral inability teaches that man is a sinner, altogether a sinner, and nothing but a sinner. As such he is an unbeliever, altogether an unbeliever, and nothing but an unbeliever." (*Rational Biblical Theology of Jonathan Edwards*, vol. 3, page 60)

Our helpless condition is the result of a soul that has no source of power to do good. By the nature of our father Adam after the Fall we are in a sad state, a state of weakness and no strength to do what is right in the eyes of God.

Rational people cannot atone themselves. They cannot propitiate God, because they are evil creatures without Christ. Unbelievers cannot regenerate their own hearts, because they are dead in their sins. An ungodly generation does not need to hear God loves them and therefore they should live good lives. They need to hear that ungodliness is the same as lawlessness, a message the church desperately needs to hear. They need to hear they are weaklings when it comes to keeping the Law of God. They need to hear they have no strength to save themselves; they are condemned and without hope unless they believe and repent. They need to hear while they were without any moral ability and had no strength to please God, yes, even while they were in the ungodly state of being Christ died for the sake of His people. Christ died for those who were legally and morally bankrupt. They had nothing to give. Their contribution was zero. Those are the kind of people who hear the gospel message. Without Christ there is no justification, there is no peace and there is no love of God.

19. Justified by the Blood of Jesus

Romans 5:9-11

The wrath of the Lord is a common expression in the Bible. It is an expression of God's anger to the sons of disobedience. Before the fall of Jerusalem the Israelites "mocked the messengers of God, despised His words, and scoffed at His prophets, until the wrath of the Lord arose against His people. . ." (2 Chronicles 36:16) .

In the gospel of John the wrath of God is particularly ever-present upon unbelievers. "He who believes in the Son has everlasting life; and he who does not believe the Son shall not see life, but the wrath of God abides on him" (John 3:36).

Paul told the Ephesians "you were once darkness" and warned them to "have no fellowship with the unfruitful works of darkness..." (Ephesians 5:8, 11). Darkness is a symbol of Satan and his angels, a symbol that is associated with words like sin, disobedience, rebellion, ignorance, blindness, falsehood, hatred, wrath, shame, strife, and bondage. The wrath of God has as its subjects all unrighteousness. Without justification the wrath of God will be the eternal condition of the unbeliever.

The blood of Christ was the instrument (or means) that obtained the believer's justification and right standing before God. The blood of Christ is central to the whole plan of salvation (Romans 3:23-25). The blood of Christ is the source of eternal life for the believer.

Paul could have emphasized the holiness and obedience of Christ, the resurrection of Christ, but no, Paul emphasized the blood of Christ. The emphasis on the blood of Christ leads to the substitutionary and sacrificial atonement of Christ. The shedding of the blood of Christ is the source of the believer's justification.

For the unbeliever moral actions will determine his standing before God. The Christian can quickly answer that the moral condition of all men, is a hopeless case. No one keeps the Law of God perfectly, save the Lord Jesus Christ. The book of James posits, "For whoever shall keep the whole Law and yet stumble in one point, he is guilty of all (2:10)." The moral condition of every person condemns that person to eternal damnation.

Paul tells us that the enemy is an ungodly man without strength, so he cannot help himself out of his ungodly mess. One of the marks of an enemy is alienation. There is discord, bitterness and ultimately hatred. Such is the language of the Apostle Paul to the Ephesian Church: "you, once Gentiles in the flesh...were without Christ, being aliens from the commonwealth of Israel" (Ephesians 2:11ff). And to the Colossian church Paul wrote, "you who once were alienated and enemies in your mind. . ." (Colossians 1:21).

The popular religious culture often thinks in fragile human terms when using words like love, hate, good, bad, or even a word like enemy. Human affections take over. Paul told the Colossians that natural man is alienated from God and natural man's mind is hostile to God. The soul must be the object of Paul's attention. How could man be hostile in mind, but not in his will? In Matthew 22:37 Jesus said, "You shall love the Lord you God with all your heart, and with all your soul, and with all your mind." Natural man is an enemy of God because natural man has a soul that does not like God. Natural man knows God but holds God's invisible attributes in derision (Romans 1:20-21).

Omniscience - Natural man does not like the idea of being intimately known by God or anyone else. Remember what happened to Adam immediately after he sinned in the garden. He covered himself up. He hid from God. Adam didn't want God to know him.

Omnipotent - Natural man does not like authority, therefore any authority figure that has power over its subject becomes the object of hate.

Immutability - Natural man cannot stand the idea that a holy God would never change His mind about eternal condemnation and punishment.

Natural man hates what he knows about God! He hates God! He represses any knowledge of God! He suppresses the truth about God! He diverts his attention therefore to man-made gods who will entertain his evil notions. Natural man loves and worships money, material things, recreation, church and many other idols. He hates God because he cannot manipulate God. He hates God because he cannot exercise his power and will over God's power and will. Unbelievers are absolutely and totally enemies of God. They show it in their thoughts and actions.

The idea of an enemy works both ways. God sees man as the enemy. The Bible is clear that God hates his enemies. The wisdom writer says God hates 7 things:

A proud look.
A lying tongue.
Hands that shed innocent blood.
A heart that devises wicked plans.
Feet that are swift in running to evil.
A false witness who speaks lies.
One who sows discord among brethren.
(Proverbs 6:16-19)

Since sin cannot be separated from the sinner, God hates the sinner. At the same time the sinner hates the strictness of God's Law. God hates the sinner and the sinner hates God. That is what Paul means when he says "we were enemies." The outcome is unbelievers are condemned to everlasting punishment and believers are saved for a favorable eternal inheritance in the presence of God.

Although believers are justified by His blood, they are reconciled through the death of God's Son, the Lord Jesus Christ. Blood is important because the believers standing before God is the result of the blood of Christ not philosophical truth or moral influence. The death of Christ is necessary to satisfy God's wrath.

By his blood Christ ransomed and freed the church, the new people of God, from the power of the evil and all evil powers (Acts 20:28; Ephesians 1:7; 1 Peter 1:18 f.; Revelation 5:9). Christ's sacrificial blood justifies all who appropriate for themselves his sacrificial death (Romans 3:25; 5:19). The blood cleanses the members of the church from their sins. God blots out the entire guilt of the person who confesses his sins to him in faithful trust (1 John 1:7-10; Revelation 1:5; 7:14). Because the blood of Christ avails for his church, it is again possible to have a clear conscience before God (Hebrews 9:14; 10:22; 13:18). (*Dictionary of New Testament Theology*, vol. 1, p. 223)

The only hope of salvation is to be justified by the blood of Christ. The satisfaction of God's justice is the central issue. The result of justification leads to sanctification, but justification was not for the purpose of exhibiting some kind of moral excellence as an example for men to follow. Paul places justification as a past action and the result of that past action there will be a future action, "we shall be saved...through Him."

All rational creatures are at war with God and the only hope is that God will change the relationship so peace will be the result. If you have peace with God you have every reason to rejoice. The grace of justification finds its ultimate joy in the grace of reconciliation and ultimate eternal peace.

20. Relationship of One to the Many

Romans 5:12-21

Although sin, death, and justification are evident doctrines throughout the book of Romans, Paul shows in this brief text the relationship of sin to death. Believers need to understand the universal nature of sin and death to understand the absolute necessity of justification. Paul does this by examining the Word of God.

There are four dimensions of Romans 5:12 that show the universal effect of sin:

Sin entered into the world.

Death entered through sin.

Death was passed along to all men.

All have sinned.

The biblical explanation for the manner in which sin entered into the world is "through one man sin entered the world." Before we consider the manner in which sin entered into the world we should ask why Paul begins Romans 5:12 with the word "therefore" which is normally a transitional word. This transition refers back to Romans 1:18. This is the place Paul begins to lay out in a systematic and meticulous fashion the relationship of sin and death to the doctrine of justification. God instructed the first man by unique revelation to obey divine Law, which identifies the covenant relationship (Genesis 2:17). Man broke the covenant by disobeying divine

Law (Genesis 3:6). A summary of this breach is found in 1 John 2:16:

> Boastful pride of life.

> Lust of the flesh.

> Lust of the eyes.

This disobedience introduced the doctrine of original sin; a term used by most Protestant theologians. Original sin refers to the result of the first sin. It is called original sin because it comes from the root of the human race. It is present from birth. It is the inward root of all actual sins. Original sin is a condition that produces actual sins.

Sin entered the human race through one man, the man Adam and Paul did say "sin entered the world." Therefore, it cannot be said that sin began with Adam, because Satan had already sinned and was the tempter for Adam. However, we can say that sin came into existence in the human race. Adam's first sin is often thought of as the Achilles heel of Christianity. (But, Christianity does not actually have an Achilles heel.) This raises the question of theodicy. It presents the problem of the origin of evil. The word theodicy derived from the Greek word *theos* meaning "God" and *dike* meaning "justice" literally means "the justice of God." It is used in debates over the origin of evil and free will. If God is totally righteous and sovereign, how could he have created a universe where evil is present? Can you choose evil without a prior desire for evil? Answer: God created Adam with a disposition that could incline itself to evil, but God is not the doer of evil.

God's sovereignty is not diminished because of evil. As Dr. John Gerstner said in one of his lectures: "God is omnipotently good and he ordains evil. It is good therefore that there should be evil." A mystery for sure, but for sure sin is an act of the creature not the creator.

Adam's sin was imputed to all his descendants. The word impute means to reckon as, credit or account to. The imputation of Adam's sin to the human race is without question. However, there is a question as to whether that imputation of Adam's in that Paul speaks of is mediate or immediate.

Mediate imputation teaches that all human beings derive a corrupt nature from Adam. To put it another way, they inherited Adam's depravity. Immediate imputation teaches that the guilt of Adam's first sin is immediately imputed to all human beings. You ask, what difference does it make? To the average person, not much. To theologians, theological professors, and ultimately pastors, the difference between mediate and immediate imputation is critical. It distinguishes between becoming a sinner, which is mediate, or being a sinner, which is immediate.

The guilt of Adam's sin was immediately imputed to the whole human race. This is the purest form of what is known as the relationship of the one to the many:

> One sin
> One time
> One representative
>
> Spread throughout
>
> By many sins
> During many times
> To all human beings

Paul explains the manner by which death entered the human race. "Therefore, just as through one man sin entered the world, and death through sin, and thus death spread to all men, because all sinned..." (Romans 5:12). The language of the New Testament indicates two kinds of death:

> physical - 1 Corinthians 15:21 - "for since by a man came death, by a man also came the resurrection of the dead."

> spiritual - 2 Thessalonians 1:8,9 - "those who do not obey the gospel of our Lord Jesus...will pay the penalty of eternal destruction away from the presence of the Lord and from the glory of His power"

There is an old cliché that fits well at this point. Those who are born again by the Holy Spirit are born twice: physical and spiritual. Those who reject the gospel of God are born once, but they die twice. They die physically and spiritually, but not annihilation. Christians will experience physical death, but not spiritual death. Christians will not experience spiritual death or the second death. "For the wages of sin is death, but the free gift of God is eternal life in Christ Jesus our Lord" (Romans 6:23). Christians have been justified; Christians have eternal peace with God.

Adam was the federal representative of the human race. The law in Eden had a different effect on the human race than God's Law as it has been violated since that day. The immediate context of Romans 5:14 is federal and typological. Adam is said to be a type of Him who was to come.

Adam is a type of Christ. The word "type" refers to a mark that is reversed and inverted. So it is said that Christ is the antitype. In the type, all sin. In the antitype, some are saved from eternal damnation.

There is some speculation at this point concerning whether or not Adam knew that he was taking the human race with him in sin. As the federal sinless head he understood the consequences of his action and that is precisely his role as a type. Adam was blessed to be in the presence of God. He was not a simpleton or idiot. His rational capacities were perfect before his lapse. He was not omniscient, but he knew what he was doing and what would happen as a result.

Similarities and opposites are necessary to make sense out of our existence. Unity and diversity have long been the subject of attention among philosophers, sociologists, anthropologists, and theologians.

Therefore, the misunderstanding of the one and the many, of the universal and the particular, of being and becoming, of analytic and synthetic reasoning, of the a priori and a posteriori. The apostle Paul certainly made use of the antithesis to deal with man's dilemma. Centuries of ink have been spilled over the problem of the one and the many in both philosophical and theological thought.

The concept of the one and the many is particularly applicable in our postmodern world. Egalitarianism, multiculturalism, and pluralism are examples of how the one and the many affect our daily lives. The emphasis in each case is the contrast of the particular to the whole. Judgment is in contrast to grace. Condemnation is in contrast to justification. The contrast is with that of Adam and Christ. Implicitly, there is the comparison, but explicitly there is the contrast. Paul focuses on the differences, not the similarities of Adam and Christ.

Adam is a type of Christ and Christ is the antitype. The sin of one (Adam) had an effect on the many.

> Therefore, as through one man's offense judgment came to all men, resulting in condemnation, even so through one Man's righteous act the free gift came to all men, resulting in justification of life. (Romans 5:18)

Condemnation is the sentence and death is the penalty.

The 2nd half of verse 18 requires close exegesis: "through one Man's righteous act the free gift came to all men." Taken by itself practicing atomistic exegesis in that passage could be translated resulting in serious error. Atomistic exegesis is the mistreatment of Scripture where one is concerned with one particular word without considering the relationship of one word to the whole of Scripture. There are 3 ways to interpret the text while consulting the whole counsel of God.

1. All men are saved.

2. Christ made salvation possible for all men.

3. All men refers to all the elect.

Dismiss 1 with 2 Thessalonians 1:3-9
Dismiss 2 with Acts 20:28 and Matthew 26:28

Those who believe that Christ only made salvation possible argue from the silence as the specificity of the elect. In other words, they would say the Bible does not specifically say that Christ did not die for the non-elect. Dr. John Gerstner explained their logic:

Christ died to make all men savable.

Dead men cannot be made savable without being made alive.

Therefore, Christ died for the salvation of no man.

Obviously "all men" referred to in Romans 5:18 does not have every human being in mind. How do we explain? The clear teaching of Scripture is that "all men" must refer to all those who belong to Christ (1 Corinthians 15:22). The language, the syntax, the context nor the doctrine demands that the same number who are condemned are the same number that are redeemed. The "righteous act" of this verse comes into question, not as it pertains to a specific number of people, but the one righteous act. The question is: what was the righteous act?

It may be argued justification is the righteous act or it may be argued that the complete work of Christ encompasses the righteous act. One Man's righteousness is the complete work of Christ, which justifies the sinner.

Whereas sin condemns the justified sinner, he or she is pardoned by the great abundance of God's grace. Sin and death are like tyrants, but justification and righteousness are eternally abundant to those who have peace with God through the Lord Jesus Christ.

21. Relationship of Justification to Sanctification

A serious error today among evangelical Christians is the mistaken idea that justification is salvation. Justification is only one aspect of God's redemptive plan. God's plan of salvation does not change. Romans chapter 5 ends with the assurance that God has declared the sinner righteous, so that grace might reign through righteousness to eternal life through Jesus Christ the Lord.

Romans chapter 6 and 7 teaches the relationship of justification to sanctification. The *Westminster Larger Catechism* defines sanctification with a brief, but biblical answer.

> Sanctification is a work of God's grace, whereby they whom God hath, before the foundation of the world, chosen to be holy, are in time, through the powerful operation of his Spirit applying the death and resurrection of Christ unto them, renewed in their whole man after the image of God; having the seeds of repentance unto life, and all other saving graces, put into their hearts, and those graces so stirred up, increased, and strengthened, as that they more and more die unto sin, and rise unto newness of life.

The *Westminster Confession of Faith* gives a terse, but simple biblical answer to the question: How are God's justified people supposed to live?

> They, who are once effectually called, and regenerated, having a new heart, and a new spirit created in them,

are further sanctified, really and personally, through the virtue of Christ's death and resurrection, by His Word and Spirit dwelling in them: the dominion of the whole body of sin is destroyed, and the several lusts thereof are more and more weakened and mortified; and they more and more quickened and strengthened in all saving graces, to the practice of true holiness, without which no man shall see the Lord.

The doctrine of sanctification is expressed as a work of God's grace. The Bible teaches that "it is God who works in you both to will and to do for His good pleasure" (Philippians 2:13).

The concept of sanctification is expressed as a progressive process where the converted sinner is "enabled more and more to die unto sin and live unto righteousness." The act of justification declares a person righteous, but that does not mean that sin is eradicated. The Reformers reply was *simul iustus et peccator*, at once righteous and a sinner. Dr. G. C. Berkouwer explains this concept:

The believer, says Luther, is like a sufferer of some disease who has been told by his physician that he will surely be cured. Hence the believer is both ill and well - but only well in the prediction of the doctor. The ill person expects complete recovery, not because he feels restoring forces at work in his body, but because he relies on a promise. So the significance of 'being righteous and at the same time a sinner' [means] believers are involved in a process of recovery and hence Luther can speak of being in part justified, in part sinner. (*Faith and Sanctification*, by G. C. Berkouwer, p. 72)

Sanctification must be viewed in its perfected form in glory even though the imperfections plague Christians throughout their lives.

The *Westminster Larger Catechism* further explains how justification and sanctification differ.

> Although sanctification be inseparably joined with justification, yet they differ, in that God in justification imputes the righteousness of Christ; in sanctification his Spirit infuses grace, and enables to the exercise thereof; in the former, sin is pardoned; in the other, it is subdued: the one doth equally free all believers from the revenging wrath of God, and that perfectly in this life, that they never fall into condemnation; the other is neither equal in all, nor in this life perfect in any, but growing up to perfection.

The doctrine of justification and sanctification has suffered because preachers and teachers have failed to communicate to the pew that both doctrines are sovereignly administered by God either justification as an act or sanctification a work. Scripture tells us that Jesus Christ became our "righteousness and sanctification" applied to the sinner for the glory of God. Through several generations preachers have focused on man doing good (moralism) rather than man being good (Christianity). Professor John Murray puts a little twist to the Reformed doctrine of sanctification.

> When we speak of sanctification we generally think of it as that process by which the believer is gradually transformed in heart, mind will, and conduct, and conformed more and more to the will of God and to the image of Christ. It is biblical to apply the term 'sanctification' to this process of transformation and conformation. But it is a fact too frequently overlooked

that in the New Testament the most characteristic terms that refer to sanctification are used, not of a process, but of a once-for-all definitive act. (*John Murray Works*, Vol. 2, p. 277).

Justification is perfection forensically applied to the sinner in this life and sanctification is the moral perfection anticipated in the life to come. Justification prepares the sinner to begin the process of sanctification or "growing up to perfection." Sanctification and holiness cannot be separated. As the writer of Hebrews said: "no one will see the Lord without sanctification or holiness" (Hebrews 12:14).

Often the word holiness is used to describe a life of sanctification. Jonathan Edwards often used the word holiness in association with sanctification. This quote from Jonathan Edwards *Miscellanies* shows the connection.

> a. OF HOLINIESS.' Holiness is a most beautiful and lovely thing. We drink in strange notions of holiness from our childhood, as if it were a melancholy, morose, sour and unpleasant thing; but there is nothing in it but what is sweet and ravishingly lovely. 'Tis the highest beauty and amiableness, vastly above all other beauties. 'Tis a divine beauty, makes the soul heavenly and far purer than anything here on earth; this world is like mire and filth and defilement to that soul which is sanctified. 'Tis of a sweet, pleasant, charming, lovely, amiable, delightful, serene, calm and still nature. 'Tis almost too high a beauty for any creatures to be adorned with; it makes the soul a little, sweet and delightful image of the blessed Jehovah.

> Oh, how may angels stand, with pleased, delighted and charmed eyes, and look and look, with smiles of

pleasure upon their lips, upon that soul that is holy; how may they hover over such a soul, to delight to behold such loveliness! How is it above all the heathen virtues, of a more light, bright and pure nature, more serene and calm, more peaceful and delightsome! What a sweet calmness, what a calm ecstasy, doth it bring to the soul! How doth it make the soul love itself; how doth it make the pure invisible world love it; yea, how doth God love it and delight in it; how do even the whole creation, the sun, the fields and trees love a humble holiness; how doth all the world congratulate, embrace, and sing to a sanctified soul!

Oh, of what a sweet, humble nature is holiness! How peaceful and, loving all things but sin, of how refined and exalted a nature is it! How doth it change the soul and make it more excellent than other beings! How is it possible that such a divine thing should be on earth? It makes the soul like a delightful field or garden planted by God, with all manner of pleasant flowers growing in the order in which nature has planted them, that is all pleasant and delightful, undisturbed, free from all the noise of man and beast, enjoying a sweet calm and the bright, calm, and gently vivifying beams of the sun forevermore: where the sun is Jesus Christ; the blessed beams and calm breeze, the Holy Spirit; the sweet and delightful flowers, and the pleasant shrill music of the little birds, are the Christian graces. Or like the little white flower: pure, unspotted and undefiled, low and humble, pleasing and harmless; receiving the beams, the pleasant beams of the serene sun, gently moved and a little shaken by a sweet breeze, rejoicing as it were in a calm rapture, diffusing around [a] most delightful fragrancy, standing most peacefully and lovingly in the midst of the other like flowers round about. How calm and serene is the heaven overhead! How free is the world from noise and disturbance! How, if one were but holy enough, would they of themselves [and] as it were naturally ascend from the earth in delight, to enjoy God as Enoch did!

The distinction must be made again and again that there is a difference between our standing before God and our actions before God. Does our standing with God mean that we are to continue in sin that grace might increase? To put it another way: What is the relationship between this justification and the life that follows? All of evangelical Christianity teaches that we are justified by faith. Probably the largest part of evangelical Christianity believes that good works, that is keeping the Law of God, is not necessary. A small percentage of evangelical Christianity believes that good works are necessary, but not meritorious. Christians have to be careful not to sever justification and sanctification. Justification is one doctrine and sanctification is another. Both are essential to the doctrine of salvation, but yet they are inseparably connected. When we combine the grammar, the context, and the profoundly metaphorical language in Romans chapter 6, we find Paul speaking about the effect and relationship of justification on sanctification. Being dead to sin carries with it two specific ideas:

1) One is definitive and all-inclusive.

2) The other is progressive and restricted to the obligation to keep the Law of God.

The Christian is dead to sin because of the blessed condition of his soul. Then the Christian has an obligation to stop practicing sin. Sin is no longer the lord of life. The dominion of sin no longer owns the soul.

For the believer, the life of sin has ended and the life of grace becomes the compelling reason to love God's Law and keep it.

Paul/James Controversy

The question of the Paul/James controversy caused so much conflict that some people actually question the authority of Scripture. The way Paul uses the word "justification" and way James uses the word "justification" appears to be contradictory. The following comparison may be helpful. The idea for this summary was derived from a course I took from Dr. Richard Belcher on the book of James at Columbia International University.

This is what James says:

James 2:14 - can faith save a man?
James 2:17 - faith is dead without works
James 2:21,22 - Abraham was justified by works
James 2:24 - by works a man is justified
James 2:24 - Rahab was justified by works

This is what Paul says:

Romans 3:21,22 - Justification is apart from works
Romans 3:24 - justification is freely by his grace
Romans 3:28 - justification is by faith
Romans 4:5 - justification is to him that works not
Galatians 2:16 - justification is not by works, but by faith
Titus 3:5 - justification is not by works of righteousness

If you impose the meaning of the words justification, faith, and works on Paul, a contradiction will result. Consider carefully how each one uses those words separately.

Paul's use of the word justification: The problem that concerns Paul is man's guilt before God and man's lack of righteousness in Romans:

1:18 - the wrath of God is revealed against men
1:32 the judgment of God
2:1 - man is without excuse before God
2:2 - the judgment of God
2:3 - no one can escape judgment
2:5 - man stores up wrath
2:12 - man will perish
2:16 - God will judge the secrets of men

Man's guilt naturally leads to the question of man's standing before God. Paul's concern is for man to have a right standing before God in Romans: therefore, removing man's guilt.

3:21 - the righteousness of God revealed
3:22 - righteousness of God through faith in Christ
3:26 - that He (Christ) might be just and the justifier of the one who has faith in Jesus
4:3 - Abraham believed God and it was accounted (credited, counted, reckoned, and imputed) to him for righteousness

Paul's solution is justification before God by faith. Paul's definition of faith is the act of the whole man. Faith includes the mind, the will, and the emotions.

Paul's use of the word works. Paul's solution speaks of justification before God apart from man's works. This means:

Works does not produce salvation
Faith precedes salvation and works follow
Not works preceding salvation
Not a combination of works and faith preceding salvation

Paul does not mean that salvation can exist without works, but the works follow justification. If we take Paul's definition of the words (justification, faith, and works) and place them on James, we face a contradiction in the Bible.

Now examine James's Teaching on Justification, faith and works.

We must see how James uses the word justification and not force Paul's definition of them. James 2:14-16 deals with a test, a test of one's real faith. Therefore, James is concerned about justification as a declaration of one's righteousness before man. This is illustrated in the life of Abraham.

Was not Abraham justified by works, when he offered up Isaac his son on the altar? If, in fact, Abraham was justified by works he had something to boast about before men, but not before God (Romans 4:2). Study the life of Abraham:

Gen. 12 - went to Egypt - lack of faith
Gen. 12 - lied while in Egypt - lack of faith
Gen. 16 - adultery with Hagar - lack of faith
Gen. 17 - laughed at God - lack of faith
Gen. 20 - lapse at Gerar - lack of faith

Genesis 22 - The evidence of Abraham's faith was manifest for the entire world to see when he offered Isaac.

James 2:22 Do you see that faith was working together with his works, and by works faith was made perfect? A better translation of the words "made perfect" is:

Consummated
Brought to its end
Brought to its goal
Reached its full development

James does not say that Abraham was saved by works, but that Abraham's saving faith was brought to the end intended by God as it produced true Christian works.

God does not save us, just to save us. God's final intent is that we live godly lives and produce Christian works for His glory. James is concerned with false faith, which is only mental assent. Demons can give mental assent, but they cannot trust God. James teaches that works is the true proof of one's faith.

2:14 - What use is it my brethren if a man says he has faith, but he has no works (true Christian works)
2:17 - Even so faith, if it has no works (true Christian works) is dead being by itself.
2:18 - I will show you my faith by my works (true Christian works)
2:26 - For just as the body without the spirit is dead so also faith without works (true Christian works) is dead.

Likewise, Jonathan Edwards believed that if man did not have true faith he could not bear "moral fruit."

Summary of the way Paul and James use the words, justification, faith, and works:

James	Paul
Justification	Justification
Before Man	Before God
Faith	Faith
true and false	full-orbed saving
Works	Works
true Christian works as	of the Law to gain
evidence of salvation	merit before God

In Romans and Galatians Paul deals with the legal and judicial aspects of the order of salvation.

James deals with faith and works from the various moral aspects.

About the Author

Martin Murphy has a B.A. in Bible from Columbia International University and Master of Divinity from Reformed Theological Seminary. Martin spent nearly thirty years in the class room, the pulpit, the lectern, the study, and the library. He now devotes most of his time consolidating academic and practical gains by writing Christian books. He is the author of twenty Christian books on topics such as apologetics, theology, and biblical exposition. He and his wife Mary live in Dothan, Alabama.

More Books by Martin Murphy

The Church: First Thirty Years, 344 pages, ISBN 9780985618179, $15.95
This book is an exposition of the Book of Acts. It will help Christians understand the purpose, mission, and ministry of the church.

The Dominant Culture: Living in the Promised Land, 172 pages, ISBN 970991481118, $11.95
This book examines the culture of Israel during the period of the Judges. It explains how worldviews influence the church and it reveals biblical principles to help Christians learn how to live in the culture.

My Christian Apology, 98 pages, ISBN 9780984570874, $7.95
This book investigates the doctrine of Christian apologetics. It explains rational Christian apologetics.

The Essence of Christian Doctrine, 200 pages, ISBN 9780984570812, $12.95

This book was written so that pastors and layman would have a quick reference to major biblical doctrines. Dr. Steve Brown says it was written, "with clarity and power about the verities of the Christian faith and in a way that makes a difference in how we live."

Return to the Lord, 130 pages, ISBN 9780984570805, $8.95

This book is an exposition of Hosea. The prophet speaks a message of repentance and hope. Hosea's prophetic message to Old Testament and New Testament congregation is "you have broken God's covenant; return to the Lord. Dr. Richard Pratt said "We need more correct and practical instruction in the prophetic books, and you have given us just that."

Theological Terms in Layman Language, 130 pages, ISBN 9780985618155, $8.95

This book is written so that simple words like faith or not so simple words like aseity are explained in plain language. Theological Terms in Layman Language is easy to read and designed for people who want a brief definition for theological terms. The terms are in layman friendly language.

Brief Study of the Ten Commandments, 164 pages, 9780991481163, $10.95

This book will help Christians discover or re-discover the meaning of the Ten Commandments.

The Present Truth, 164 pages, ISBN 9780983244172, $8.95

Each chapter examines a topic relative to the Christian life. Topics such as church, sin, anger, marriage, education and more.

Doctrine of Sound Words: Summary of Christian Theology, 424 pages, ISBN 9780991481125, $16.95

This explains the doctrine of Christianity in a systematic format for the layperson. It covers a wide range of theological topics such as, the triune God, creation, providence, sin, justification, repentance, Christian liberty, free will, marriage and divorce, Christian fellowship, et al). There are thirty three topics beginning with "Holy Scriptures" and ending with "The Last Judgment." It is a systematic theology for laymen based on the full counsel of God.

The god of the Church Growth Movement, 95 pages ISBN 9780986405587, $6.95

This work includes a brief explanation of modernity and its effect on church growth. It is a critical analysis of the church growth movement found in every branch of the Protestant church.

Friendship: The Joy of Relationships, 46 pages, ISBN 9780986405518, $6.49

This condensed book was written so the reader will be able to grasp the principles without having to go back and re-read it to digest the content. Friendship is a popular concept. Having a large number of friends was popularized by the social media such as Twitter and Facebook. Friendship involves a relationship of distinction. It is a relationship that respects the dignity of another person. The Bible teaches a different version of what it means to be a friend than the popular culture teaches.

Ultimate Authority for the Soul, 151 pages, ISBN 9780986405501, $9.99

This book examines that question and concludes that every rational being has some recognition of God as the ultimate authority. Although God is the ultimate authority, He confers His authority by means of the Word of God. The author examines Psalm 119 to build a defense for the ultimate authority for the soul.

Constitutional Authority in a Postmodern Culture, ISBN 9780985618124, 56 pages, $5.95

This book shows the validity of constitutional authority and the invasion of postmodern theories in western culture. Postmodern theory has assaulted the western culture on the battleground of absolute truth and reality. Postmodern theory places human experience over abstract objective principles. Christians have a constitution known as the Bible so they will know the truth of reality. The last chapter is devoted to cultural reformation.

Learn to Pray: Biblical Doctrine of Prayer, ISBN 9780986405563, 107 pages, $7.95.

This book examines the Lord's model prayer so Christians may learn to pray according to the Lord's instruction. It also reviews some of the prayers of the apostle Paul to discover his doctrine of prayer. Pastor James Perry wrote the Foreword with insight and experience. "I am impressed with this book on the subject of Learn to Pray. It is stated briefly and succinctly following the model and example of the Lord's Prayer. There is considerable practical instruction on the meaning and implication about purposeful and biblical prayer and it will serve as a useful primer for all who apply the prayer principles. The reader will doubtlessly return to the instruction frequently for the practical help it offers."

www.ingramcontent.com/pod-product-compliance
Lightning Source LLC
Chambersburg PA
CBHW070205060426
42445CB00033B/1553